Hans-Philipp Otto

Essays on the Saudi Stock Exchange

Hans-Philipp Otto

Essays on the Saudi Stock Exchange

Market Efficiency, Active Investment Strategies and Sectoral Dependency on Oil Price

Tectum Verlag

The Deutsche Nationalbibliothek lists this publication in the Deutsche Nationalbibliografie; detailed bibliographic data are available on the Internet at http://dnb.d-nb.de

ISBN 978-3-8288-4682-1 (Print)
978-3-8288-7765-8 (ePDF)

a.t.: EBS Universität für Wirtschaft und Recht, Diss., 2021

Submitted under the title:

"Essays on the Saudi Stock Exchange
How informational efficient is the Saudi Stock Exchange?
How successful are active portfolio investment strategies for the Saudi Stock Exchange?
How dependent are Saudi Arabia's economic sectors on oil price?"

British Library Cataloguing-in-Publication Data
A catalogue record for this book is available from the British Library.

ISBN 978-3-8288-4682-1 (Print)
978-3-8288-7765-8 (ePDF)

Library of Congress Cataloging-in-Publication Data
Otto, Hans-Philipp
Essays on the Saudi Stock Exchange
Market Efficiency, Active Investment Strategies
and Sectoral Dependency on Oil Price
144 pp.
Includes bibliographic references.

ISBN 978-3-8288-4682-1 (Print)
978-3-8288-7765-8 (ePDF)

1st edition 2022

Printed and bound in Germany.

Acknowledgments

Dear reader,

I would like to thank the people who made this dissertation possible.

Professor Dr. Ferdinand Mager, who guided and encouraged me throughout the whole process with advice and expertise giving me the opportunity to graduate at his chair.

Professor Sandra Paterlini, PhD, whose ideas and feedback contributed significantly to this dissertation.

The staff and fellow students at EBS, who made the process smooth and provided new perspectives.

Daniel Jakubowski, with whom I started to work with MATLAB during our master's degree and who provided the raw data.

Dr. Benjamin Ruf, who challenged me and was a great counterpart for discussions.

My family, especially my parents Barbara and Hans-Joachim Otto, who made me strive and believed in me while providing sustained support and stability.

Contents

List of Tables

List of Figures

1. Introduction

The Saudi Stock Exchanges (Tadawul) was, in December 2019, at the center of attention of world finance. The initial public offering (IPO) of the country's national oil company, Aramco, was the largest in terms of size and company valuation worldwide, making the Tadawul the ninth largest capital market in the world in terms of market capitalization. In preparation for the Aramco IPO, the Tadawul amplified its efforts to enhance its structural and regulatory framework toward international stock exchange standards, to make the Tadawul more attractive to foreign investors. Examples of the actions taken include opening the market to foreign institutional investors (2015), reclassifying subindices in accordance with the Global Industry Classification Standard (GICS) (2017), shifting to a two-day settlement cycle (2017), and joining the MSCI Emerging Markets index (2018) followed by the FTSE Russell and S&P DJI Emerging Markets indexes (2019). These developments are aided by new corporate governance rules, a new delivery versus payment model, and the introduction of stock borrowing, lending, and short-selling, moving toward a more efficient stock market under international standards.

The first paper in this cumulative dissertation, "How informational efficient is the Saudi Stock Exchange?", focuses on the weak-form market efficiency hypothesis, a major research area focusing on better understanding and promoting the quality of financial markets, as efficient stock markets signal a resilient economy. Efficient markets also indicate investor confidence in the macroeconomic fundamentals of an economy, as inefficient markets struggle with illiquidity, lack of transparency, herding behavior, insider trading, and other structural deficits. From 2007 to 2017, using a large variety of test methods, we find that the Tadawul All Share Index (TASI), along with all its subindices, are not weak-form market efficient; however, they do not exhibit long-range dependency. Further, an enhancement of the degree of efficiency could not be detected.

The starting point of the second paper, "How successful are active portfolio investment strategies for the Saudi Stock Exchange?", are market inefficiencies in the Tadawul detected in the first paper. The main research aim is to test whether these inefficiencies can be exploited using active investment strategies based on mechanical trading rules to outperform the market on a systematic basis and generate abnormal risk-adjusted returns while maintaining a well-diversified portfolio. The investigation proceeds according to the hypothesis that there is an interrelation between the degree of weak-form market efficiency, in terms of time period as well as data frequency, and the magnitude of outperformance of active investment strategies. We apply a selection of quantitative asset allocation strategies on the 15 TASI subindices in the timeframe 2007 to 2017 and show that the inefficiencies of the Tadawul can be transformed into abnormal risk-adjusted returns. However, direct alignment of the graduated degree of market efficiency and the ability to predict future prices from past price changes could not be confirmed with the applied data segmentation.

The third paper, "How dependent are the different economic sectors in Saudi Arabia on the oil price?", anticipates a dynamic relation between the Tadawul and oil prices, given the importance of Saudi Arabia as an oil exporting country. However, this relation also serves as an indicator of the diversification and resilience of Saudi Arabia's economy, aiding investor confidence in the macroeconomic fundamentals of the economy. Therefore, the Government of Saudi Arabia has amplified its efforts to gradually gain independence from oil export revenues with programs such as the National Transformational Program 2020. Using correlation and cointegration analysis, in the time period 2007 to 2017, we find a strong and significant relation between crude oil prices and the TASI, as well as the petro sector. Further, we provide empirical evidence from economic sectors that are to a great extent long- and short-term independent from oil price developments. Over time, the relation between the Tadawul and crude oil prices intensifies from both a short- and long-term perspective.

In a broader sense and apart from political stability, these three papers aim to answer the most critical questions concerning investment decisions in the Tadawul: What is the quality of the financial market? Can active investment strategies outperform the market on a systematic and continuing basis? How oil-dependent is the Saudi economy?

All papers presented in the cumulative dissertation are organized as follows. Section 1 presents a literature review. Section 2 presents the data description and the methodology. Section 3 presents the empirical results together with an evaluation and discussion. Finally, section 4 concludes. For reference, one joint literature list is provided.

2. How informational efficient is the Saudi Stock Exchange?

This paper analyzes and extends the literature on the efficient market hypothesis as applied to the Tadawul. Firstly, it covers the largest dataset of the Tadawul, including 15 subindices. Secondly, it tests the index on a sectoral level. Thirdly, the paper embodies an exhaustive number of test methods. Finally, it focuses on possible temporal developments. We find that the TASI and all subindices are not weak-form market efficient. However, the TASI and all its subindices do not exhibit long-range dependency. Further, an enhanced degree of efficiency is not found.

2.1 Literature review

Capital market efficiency describes several distinct but interrelated concepts, including allocational, operational, and informational efficiency (Fama, 1998; Brown, 1988). In general, most empirical studies on financial market efficiency are concerned with informational efficiency (Jarrow & Larsson, 2012). The theoretical foundation for informational efficiency was laid by Regnault (1863) and Bachelier (1900) and expanded by Kendal (1953), Cootner (1962), Osborne (1962), Samuelson (1965), and Mandelbrot (1966) before being reviewed and consolidated by Fama (1970) in the efficient market hypothesis, which derives three distinct gradations: weak, semi-strong, and strong forms, according to the level of information being considered (Al Janabi, Hatemi-J, & Irandoust, 2010). The weak form is defined as the state where stock prices completely reflect all current available information and are consequently not influenced by past events (Malkiel, 2003; Fama, 1970). The examination whether a stock market is weak-form efficient is based on the random walk hypothesis determining that successive price changes are identically distributed and independent (Fama, 1970). Accepting weak-form market efficiency implies that there is no arbitrage opportunity for investors to make excess abnormal profit based on analysis of past return information (Risso, 2008; Jensen, 1978). In contrast, inefficient markets are characterized by distortions in the pricing of capital and risk, inhibiting efficient allocation of capital (Jamaani & Roca, 2015). Therefore, weak-form efficiency is a desirable characteristic for financial markets to achieve, particularly for emerging markets competing in a global economy (Budd, 2012), where generally the idea of a departure from weak efficiency is supported (Abdmoulah, 2010); this has been a major research area for evaluating the quality of financial markets (Arshad, Rizvi, Ghani, & Duasa, 2016).

Recent literature focusing on market efficiency and the Tadawul is shaped mainly by ranking a subset of Middle Eastern indices according to their degree of efficiency using only a small range of testing methods and with data up to 2013 (Mensi, Tiwari, & Yoon, 2017). A tendency to reject the weak-form market hypothesis for the Tadawul (Arshad, Rizvi, Ghani, & Duasa, 2016; Charfeddine & Khediri, 2016; Jamaani & Roca, 2015; Sensoy, 2013) is common in the literature (Budd, 2012; Al-Ajmi & Kim, 2012; Al Ashikh, 2012; Abdmoulah, 2010). Taking the only two papers into consideration that tested the weak-form efficient market hypothesis for the subindices of the Tadawul, the results remain uncertain and divergent even though the research was conducted using similar datasets and partially overlapping methods (Asiri & Alzeera, 2013; Budd, 2012). The compilation in Table 1 below provides a thorough overview of the literature on weak-form market efficiency with a focus on the Tadawul.

Author	Year	Journal	Data from Saudi Arabia	Length	Fre-quenzy	Methods	Results
Butler and Malaikah	1992	Journal of Banking & Finance(16)	35 stocks from SSE	1985-1989	Daily	Serial correlation and runs tests	Rejection of random walk hypothesis
Al-Razeen	1997	PhD Thesis, University of Leicester	28 stocks from SSE	1992-1995	Weekly	Serial correlation, runs, and filter rules tests	Low level of weak form efficiency
Khababa	1998	Journal of Financial Management and Analysis(11)	61 stocks from SSE	1985-1997	Weekly	Autocorrelation and runs tests	High level of serial dependence
Dahel and Laabas	1999	Economic Research Forum for the Arab Countries	Saudi Stock index	1994-1998	Weekly	Augmented Dickey-Fuller, the Phillips-Perron, the variance ratio, and autocorrelation tests	Stock index of Saudi Arabia is characterized by weak form efficiency
Alkholifey	2000	PhD Thesis, Colorado State University	Not available	Not available	Not available	Autocorrelation, filter rules, runs, and the cointegration test	Rejection of informationally efficient market
Abraham et al.	2002	Financial Review(37)	Saudi Stock index	1992-1998	Weekly	Variance ratio and the runs tests	No rejection of random walk hypothesis
Onour	2004	Ministry of Economy and Planning, Riyadh: Saudi Arabia	Saudi Stock index and subindices of banking and cement	2003-2004	Daily	Runs and the von Neumann tests	Rejection of weak form market efficiency hypothesis
Al-Abdulqader et al.	2007	Journal of Emerging Market Finance(6)	45 stocks from SSE	1990-2000	Weekly	Filter rule test and the moving average strategy	Tendency towards acceptance of efficient market hypothesis
Al-Khazali et al.	2007	The Financial Review(42)	Saudi Stock index	1994-2003	Weekly	Rank, runs, and variance ratio tests	Acceptance of efficient market hypothesis
Benjelloun and Squalli	2008	International Journal of Managerial Finance(4)	Saudi Stock index and subindices of agriculture, banking, cement, electricity, industry, and services	1990-2006	Weekly	Multiple variance ratio test (RW) and runs test (WFE)	No rejection of random walk hypothesis but rejection of weak form market efficiency hypothesis
Onour	2009	Operations Research(10)	Saudi Stock index, banking subindex and 3 stocks from SSE	2003-2006	Daily	Dickey-Fuller, Phillips-Perron, the KPSS, the variance ratio tests	Rejection of random walk hypothesis

Author	Year	Journal	Data from Saudi Arabia	Length	Fre-quenzy	Methods	Results
Abdmoulah	2010	International Review of Financial Analysis(19)	Saudi Stock index	1994-2009	Daily	GARCH-M (1,1) methodology along with state-space time-varying parameters	Rejection of weak form market efficiency hypothesis
Bley	2011	Emerging Markets Review(12)	Saudi Stock index	2000-2009 seg-mented	Daily, weekly, and monthly	Dickey-Fuller, the Phillips-Perron, the KPSS, the autocorrelation function, the Ljung-Box Q-Statistic, the variance ratio test as well as AR, ARMA, and GARCH models	Rejection of random walk hypothesis for daily data and some traces of a random walk in individual subperiods of weekly and monthly data
Al Ashikh	2012	International Review of Business Research Papers(8)	Saudi Stock index, banks and financial services subindex and 3 stocks from SSE	2000-2010	Daily	Augmented Dickey-Fuller, the Phillips-Perron, the autocorrelation function, the Ljung-Box Q-Statistic, and the runs tests	Rejection of weak form market efficiency hypothesis
Al-Ajmi and Kim	2012	Applied Economics(44)	Saudi Stock index	1999-2010	Daily and weekly	Three multiple variance ratio tests	Rejection of weak form market efficiency hypothesis
Budd	2012	Journal of Finance and Accountancy(10)	Saudi Stock index and all 15 subindices	2007-2011	Daily	Variance ratio and runs tests	Rejection of random walk hypothesis some indication of weak-form efficiency solitary for the banking, the building, the insurance and the telecommunication sector
Asiri and Alzeera	2013	Research Journal of Finance and Accounting(4)	Saudi Stock index and all 15 subindices	2006-2012 seg-mented	Daily	Dickey-Fuller, the Pearson correlation, the Durbin-Watson, and the Wald-Wolfowitz runs tests	The Tadawul All Share Index and eleven out of fifteen sectors have met the properties of weak-form efficiency (other than banks and financial services, energy and utilities, insurance, and building and construction)
Hokroh	2013	Asian Journal of Finance & Accounting(5)	Saudi Stock index	2007	Daily	Autocorrelation and the run tests	Rejection of weak form market efficiency hypothesis
Sensoy	2013	Physica A(392)	Saudi Stock index	2007-2012	Daily	Hurst exponent	Rejection of weak form market efficiency hypothesis

Author	Year	Journal	Data from Saudi Arabia	Length	Frequenzy	Methods	Results
Al Abdulhadi el al.	2015	International Journal of Business(20)	3 stocks from SSE	2005-2010	Daily	Fractal analysis	Two out of three stocks are not weak form efficient
Jamaani and Roca	2015	Research in International Business and Finance(33)	Saudi Stock index	2003-2013	Daily	Augmented Dickey-Fuller, the Phillips-Perron, the variance ratio, the multiple variance ratio, the runs, and the Wright tests	Rejection of weak form market efficiency hypothesis
Arshad et al.	2016	Research in International Business and Finance(36)	Saudi Stock index	1998-2012 segmented	Daily	Christiano–Fitzgerald filter and multifactural de-trended fluctuation analysis	Saudi Arabia is ranked in the midfield comparing weak form marekt efficiency with the other OIC countires
Charfeddine and Khediri	2016	Physica A(444)	Saudi Stock index	2005-2013	Daily	GARCH(1,1) model and detrended fluctuation analysis technique, the modified R/S statistic, the exact local whittle and the feasible Exact Local Whittle approach	Rejection of weak form market efficiency hypothesis (except GARCH(1,1))

Table 1: Market efficiency literature on Tadawul

This paper contributes to the research on market efficiency of the Tadawul from various angles, extending the empirical foundation laid by previous authors. The dataset covers the Tadawul together with its 15 subindices for the period 2007 to 2017, the longest possible timeframe for the Tadawul and its subindices framed be the reclassifications. Further, this paper enhances the validity and explanatory power of scientific research on the Tadawul from a methodological viewpoint, overcoming robustness limitations by applying a total of 12 parametric and nonparametric test methods of the weak-form market efficiency hypothesis. Accurate conclusions require a wide range of test methods due to the inherent limitations suffered by each model. Additionally, the possibility of temporal variation of the weak-form market efficiency hypothesis is tested via data segmentation and supported by the Shannon entropy test, making this the most extensive study on weak-form market efficiency of the Tadawul thus far. The efficiency of stock markets matters to academics in understanding the working mechanisms and efficiency characteristics of equity markets, to investors in identifying and understanding investment opportunities, and to policy makers in developing the stock markets of emerging countries (Jamaani & Roca, 2015; Abdmoulah, 2010).

2.2 Data and methodology

In line with the majority of research papers on market efficiency, we follow the reasoning of Fama (1970) and test whether the TASI and its 15 subindices are weak-form market efficient, as successive price changes of individual time series are identically distributed and independent random variables. Using the same approach, we split the dataset into five consecutive subsets of equal length to investigate time-dependent change in the degree of weak-form market efficiency, and combine these results with the evolution of information efficiency measured by Shannon entropy, which has a similar effect due to the rolling window.

2.2.1 Data

The input data for the empirical analysis contains the TASI and its 15 subindex datasets in daily and, for robustness reasons, weekly frequency from 06.01.2007 to 05.01.2017 (that is, until reclassification in accordance with the Global Industry Classification Standard), resulting in 2509 daily and 499 weekly time-dependent data points (Saudi Stock Exchange, 2017). Further, the dataset at daily frequency is split into five segments containing approximately 502 time-dependent data points. All datasets underlying the empirical analysis consist of financial time series common to most analysis of logarithmic asset returns (Tsay, 2005; Campbell, Lo, & MacKinlay, 1997). The sectoral overview of the 15 subindices is provided in Table 2 below (Saudi Stock Exchange, 2016).

Tadawul and subindices		
Code	Name	Nomenclature paper
SASEIDX	Tadawul	TASI
SASEBNK	Tadawul All Share Banking Index	Subindex 1
SASEPETR	Tadawul All Share Petro Index	Subindex 2
SASECEM	Tadawul All Share Cement Index	Subindex 3
SASERETL	Tadawul All Share Retail Industries Index	Subindex 4
SASEINS	Tadawul All Share Insurance Index	Subindex 5
SASETEL	Tadawul All Share Telecommunications Index	Subindex 6
SASEREAL	Tadawul All Share Real Estate Development Industries Index	Subindex 7
SASEBULD	Tadawul All Share Building & Construction Index	Subindex 8
SASEMINV	Tadawul All Share Multi-Investment Index	Subindex 9
SASEINDI	Tadawul All Share Industrial Investment Industries Index	Subindex 10
SASEAGRI	Tadawul All Share Agriculture & Food Industries Index	Subindex 11
SASEENER	Tadawul All Share Energy & Utilities Industries Index	Subindex 12
SASEMEDI	Tadawul All Share Media & Publishing Industries Index	Subindex 13
SASETRAN	Tadawul All Share Transport Industries Index	Subindex 14
SASEHOTE	Tadawul All Share Hotel & Tourism Industries Index	Subindex 15

Table 2: Subindex sectoral overview

Table 3 below reports descriptive statistics for the TASI together with its 15 subindices.

Descriptive statistics (daily 06.01.2007-05.01.2017)

	DS					
	mean return	sigma	skewness	kurtosis	Jarque-Bera test	p-value (5%)
TASI	-0.0000175	0.0063	-0.8458	12.4273	9590	0.000
Subindex 1	-0.0000665	0.0064	-0.1946	10.9742	6663	0.000
Subindex 2	0.0000089	0.0083	-0.6500	9.9022	5157	0.000
Subindex 3	-0.0000470	0.0058	-0.6741	15.4540	16405	0.000
Subindex 4	0.0001183	0.0067	-0.7657	11.7220	8198	0.000
Subindex 5	-0.0000083	0.0090	-0.8278	6.9580	1924	0.000
Subindex 6	-0.0001176	0.0067	-0.4931	10.8646	6568	0.000
Subindex 7	0.0000546	0.0077	-0.5519	9.4934	4535	0.000
Subindex 8	-0.0001585	0.0082	-1.0683	10.0268	5639	0.000
Subindex 9	-0.0001084	0.0087	-0.8376	8.9524	3997	0.000
Subindex 10	0.0000385	0.0081	-0.9226	9.3969	4634	0.000
Subindex 11	0.0000874	0.0070	-0.6030	10.3806	5847	0.000
Subindex 12	0.0000809	0.0070	0.1520	11.2466	7119	0.000
Subindex 13	-0.0001159	0.0102	0.0306	7.6273	2239	0.000
Subindex 14	0.0000739	0.0086	-0.5293	8.9525	3821	0.000
Subindex 15	0.0001019	0.0100	-0.0633	10.2998	5572	0.000

Table 3: Descriptive statistics for continuous daily dataset

The observed data are mostly negative-skewed with long left tails and high kurtosis, indicating fat tails and high peaks. The normality of the distribution is rejected by Jarque-Bera test for all indices (Jarque & Bera, 1987) and high systemic risk is presumed (Cont, Moussa, & Santos, 2013). With this in mind, the results of the parametric tests need to be assessed with caution, as the requirement that data be normally distributed is a critical limitation to parametric tests, with the possibility of constituting statistical bias to the results when absent (Guidi & Gupta, 2013).

2.2.2 Methodology

Tests for stationarity (augmented Dickey-Fuller, Phillips-Perron), autocorrelation (Durbin-Watson, autocorrelation function, variance ratio, Pearson and Spearman correlation) as well as long-range dependency (rescaled range statistic via Hurst exponent and Lo modified) are based on Lo and MacKinlay (1999), while runs test (Wald-Wolfowitz) for serial correlation and Shannon entropy test measuring information efficiency follow Fama (1965) and Risso (2009), respectively. Aggregated, these methods not only cover but extend previous studies of weak-form market efficiency conducted on the Tadawul, in both variety and validity. The extensive range of test methods employed is justified by the fact that the weak-form efficient market hypothesis is a challenging concept that is difficult to measure empirically (Mensi, Tiwari, & Yoon, 2017; Sensoy, 2013), while each method contains specific strengths and weaknesses with distinct explanatory power according to its inherent statistical properties. A detailed methodological description of the test methods is provided in the following subsections, together with the individual result tables of the continuous daily dataset. Aggregated results are provided in the results section.

2.2.2.1 Augmented Dickey-Fuller and Phillips-Perron test

The Dickey-Fuller (1979) test was developed as a procedure for testing whether a time series has a unit root or, equivalently, the time series follows a random walk. This original approach introduced the problem that the test is valid only if the time series y_t is well characterized by an autoregressive process of the first-order AR(1) with white noise errors (Harris, 1992). Said and Dickey (1984) show that a high-order autoregressive process AR(p) can be used to accommodate an unknown ARIMA process in which the order of the autoregression grows with sample size. This test is referred to as the augmented Dickey-Fuller test. The lag length in the augmented Dickey-Fuller test is set at the smallest p such that all longer lags up to p^{max} are jointly insignificant (Weber, 2001). The augmented Dickey-Fuller test with constant and linear time trend is given on estimating the test regression as follows (Harris, 1992):

$$\Delta y_t = \alpha + \beta y_{t-1} + \delta_t + \sum_{j=1}^{p} \varphi_j \Delta y_{t-j} + \epsilon_t \tag{1}$$

In the test with constant and no trend, the term δ_t is left out of the equation above, while in the test without constant and trend the term α is also absent.

The Phillips-Perron (1988) unit root test differs from the augmented Dickey-Fuller test mainly in how it addresses serial correlation and heteroskedasticity in the errors. The test utilizes the Newey-West (1987) standard errors, making the test robust to serial correlation via a nonparametric adjustment through the heteroskedasticity and autocorrelation consistent covariance matrix estimator (Fox, 1997). In addition, the Phillips-Perron test has the advantage that the lag length for the test regression does not have to be specified. The Phillips-Perron test with constant and linear time trend fits the regression:

$$\Delta y_t = \alpha + \beta y_{t-1} + \delta_t + \epsilon_t \tag{2}$$

Parallel to the Dickey-Fuller test, the variant with constant and no trend and the variant without constant and trend are considered for the Phillips-Perron test as well. The two test statistics of the Phillips-Perron test Z_ρ and Z_τ are calculated as follows:

$$Z_\rho = n\left(\hat{\rho}_n - 1\right) - \frac{1}{2}\frac{n^2\hat{\sigma}^2}{s_n^2}\left(\hat{\lambda}_n^2 - \hat{\gamma}_{0,n}\right) \tag{3}$$

$$Z_\tau = \sqrt{\frac{\hat{\gamma}_{0,n}}{\hat{\lambda}_n^2}\frac{\hat{\rho}_n - 1}{\hat{\sigma}}} - \frac{1}{2}\left(\hat{\lambda}_n^2 - \hat{\gamma}_{0,n}\right)\frac{1}{\hat{\lambda}_n}\frac{n\hat{\sigma}}{s_n} \tag{4}$$

$$\hat{\gamma}_{j,n} = \frac{1}{n}\sum_{i=j+1}^{n} \hat{v}_i \hat{v}_{i-j} \tag{5}$$

$$\hat{\lambda}_n^2 = \hat{\gamma}_{0,n} + 2\sum_{j=1}^{q}\left(1 - \frac{j}{q+1}\right)\hat{\gamma}_{j,n} \tag{6}$$

$$s_n^2 = \frac{1}{n-k}\sum_{i=1}^{n} \hat{v}_i^2 \tag{7}$$

where v is the OLS residual, k is the number of covariates in the regression, q is the number of Newey-West lags to use in calculating $\hat{\lambda}_n^2$, and $\hat{\sigma}$ is the OLS standard error of $\hat{\rho}$. The Z statistics extend the work of Phillips (1987) for the case of an autoregression with no fitted constant or time trend by correcting the conventional regression statistics for allowing the effects of serial-correlated and heterogeneously distributed innovations (Phillips & Perron, 1988).

The null hypotheses of both the augmented Dickey-Fuller and the Phillips-Perron tests are defined as:

H_0 = time series contains a unit root and is non stationary

whereas the alternative hypothesis is given by:

H_1 = times series contains no unit root and is stationary

Further, the critical values for testing the null hypothesis of the augmented Dickey-Fuller test are identical to those for the Phillips-Perron test (Fuller, 1976; Phillips & Perron, 1988). Tables 4 and 5 below show the results of the augmented Dickey-Fuller test and the Phillips-Perron test for the continuous daily dataset.

Augmented Dickey-Fuller test (daily 06.01.2007-05.01.2017)

	ADF test		
	No constant and no trend	Constant and no trend	Constant and trend
TASI	-45.2334*	-45.2245*	-45.2158*
Subindex 1	-44.4785*	-44.4732*	-44.4661*
Subindex 2	-46.6473*	-46.6381*	-46.6331*
Subindex 3	-45.3878*	-45.3815*	-45.3734*
Subindex 4	-46.3230*	-46.3283*	-46.3190*
Subindex 5	-44.4832*	-44.4743*	-44.4701*
Subindex 6	-45.6237*	-45.6267*	-45.6201*
Subindex 7	-45.8779*	-45.8715*	-45.8873*
Subindex 8	-43.6626*	-43.6670*	-43.6611*
Subindex 9	-45.9953*	-45.9921*	-45.9867*
Subindex 10	-46.6450*	-46.6371*	-46.6278*
Subindex 11	-45.2133*	-45.2110*	-45.2021*
Subindex 12	-55.8271*	-55.8257*	-55.8434*
Subindex 13	-42.3950*	-42.3906*	-42.4011*
Subindex 14	-46.9617*	-46.9562*	-46.9634*
Subindex 15	-45.4232*	-45.4182*	-45.4121*

* Indicates the rejection of the null hypothesis of a unit root and non stationarity at a 1% level of significance for values below the critical value of -2.58 (no constant and no trend), -3.43 (constant and no trend) and, -3.96 (constant and trend).

Table 4: Augmented Dickey-Fuller test

Phillips-Perron test (daily 06.01.2007-05.01.2017)

	PP test		
	No constant and no trend	Constant and no trend	Constant and trend
TASI	-45.2334*	-45.2245*	-45.2158*
Subindex 1	-44.4785*	-44.4732*	-44.4661*
Subindex 2	-46.6473*	-46.6381*	-46.6331*
Subindex 3	-45.3878*	-45.3815*	-45.3734*
Subindex 4	-46.3230*	-46.3283*	-46.3190*
Subindex 5	-44.4832*	-44.4743*	-44.4701*
Subindex 6	-45.6237*	-45.6267*	-45.6201*
Subindex 7	-45.8779*	-45.8715*	-45.8873*
Subindex 8	-43.6626*	-43.6670*	-43.6611*
Subindex 9	-45.9953*	-45.9921*	-45.9867*
Subindex 10	-46.6450*	-46.6371*	-46.6278*
Subindex 11	-45.2133*	-45.2110*	-45.2021*
Subindex 12	-55.8271*	-55.8257*	-55.8434*
Subindex 13	-42.3950*	-42.3906*	-42.4011*
Subindex 14	-46.9617*	-46.9562*	-46.9634*
Subindex 15	-45.4232*	-45.4182*	-45.4121*

* Indicates the rejection of the null hypothesis of a unit root and non stationarity at a 1% level of significance for values below the critical value of -2.58 (no constant and no trend), -3.43 (constant and no trend) and, -3.96 (constant and trend).

Table 5: Phillips-Perron test

2.2.2.2 Durbin-Watson test

The most common test for first-order autocorrelation of errors in regression models is the bounds test of Durbin and Watson (Dufour & Dagenais, 1985). The Durbin-Watson test is based on the work and distribution derived by von Neumann (Durbin & Watson, 1950), focusing on testing regression residuals for serial correlation (Habibagahi & Pratschke, 1972).

The null hypothesis of the Durbin-Watson test is defined as (Dent & Cassing, 1978):

$$H_0 = \text{time series is not autocorrelated}$$

whereas the alternative hypothesis is given by:

$$H_1 = \text{time series is autocorrelated}$$

The Durbin-Watson test statistic is given by (Durbin & Watson, 1950):

$$d = \frac{\sum_{\mu=2}^{n} \left(z_{\mu} - z_{\mu-1}\right)^{2}}{\sum_{\mu=1}^{n} z_{\mu}^{2}} \tag{8}$$

where n is the number of observations, and z_{μ} is the residual at time μ.

The Durbin-Watson d statistic can range from 0 to 4, with a center of distribution of 2. The value of $d = 0$ is given at perfect positive autocorrelation, while the value of $d = 4$ is given at perfect negative autocorrelation. The acceptance point of H_0 is given at $d = 2$ with upper and lower bounds at the 5% level of significance as established by Savin and White (1977) based on sample size and number of regressors. Table 6 below provides the results of the Durbin-Watson test for the continuous daily dataset.

Durbin-Watson test (daily 06.01.2007-05.01.2017)

	DW test	
	Durbin-Watson statistic	p-value
TASI	1.7946	0.0000*
Subindex 1	1.7604	0.0000*
Subindex 2	1.8573	0.0003*
Subindex 3	1.8043	0.0000*
Subindex 4	1.8413	0.0001*
Subindex 5	1.7645	0.0000*
Subindex 6	1.8139	0.0000*
Subindex 7	1.8217	0.0000*
Subindex 8	1.7243	0.0000*
Subindex 9	1.8287	0.0000*
Subindex 10	1.8550	0.0003*
Subindex 11	1.7955	0.0000*
Subindex 12	2.2120	0.0000*
Subindex 13	1.6680	0.0000*
Subindex 14	1.8694	0.0010*
Subindex 15	1.8057	0.0000*

* Indicates the rejection of the null hypothesis of no autocorrelation at a 1% level of significance for p-values below 0.01.

Table 6: Durbin-Watson test

2.2.2.3 Autocorrelation function test and Ljung-Box Q test

The autocorrelation function test reveals the degree of autocorrelation in a time series by measuring the correlation between the current and lagged stock returns (Box, Jenkins, Reinsel, & Ljung, 2015). While the autocorrelation function test investigates the randomness of the time series at each of the defined lags of the Ljung-Box Q test, a modification of the Box-Pierce portmanteau test (Box & Pierce, 1970) is designed to detect autocorrelation at multiple lags jointly (Ljung & Box, 1978).

The null hypothesis of the autocorrelation function test and the Ljung-Box Q test is defined as (Engle & Russel, 1998):

$$H_0 = \text{time series is not autocorrelated}$$

whereas the alternative hypothesis is given by:

$$H_1 = \text{time series is autocorrelated}$$

The calculation for the autocorrelation function test is (Box, Jenkins, Reinsel, & Ljung, 2015):

$$p_k = \frac{\sum_{t=1}^{N-k} (r_t - \bar{r})(r_{t+k} - \bar{r})}{\sum_{t=1}^{N} (r_t - \bar{r})^2} \tag{9}$$

where p_k is the serial correlation coefficient of stock returns of lag k, and N is number of observations. The following properties apply to p_k (Box, Jenkins, Reinsel, & Ljung, 2015)

$$p_0 = 1, p_k = p_{-k}, -1 \leq p_k \leq 1 \tag{10}$$

At the 5% level of significance, null hypothesis H_0 is rejected when p_k lies outside the boundaries defined as (Box, Jenkins, Reinsel, & Ljung, 2015):

$$\pm \frac{Z_{.025}}{\sqrt{N}} \tag{11}$$

The Ljung-Box test statistic is given by (Ljung & Box, 1978):

$$Q = N(N+2)\sum_{k=1}^{h}\frac{\hat{p}_k^2}{N-k} \tag{12}$$

where h is the number of lags tested.

At the 5% level of significance, null hypothesis H_0 is rejected for Q greater than the 5% quantile of the chi-squared distribution with h degrees of freedom (Ljung & Box, 1978). Tables 7 and 8 below display the results of the autocorrelation function test and the Ljung-Box Q test for the continuous daily dataset, respectively.

Autocorrelation function test (daily 06.01.2007-05.01.2017)

	ACF test				
Number of lags, k	AC k=1	AC k=2	AC k=3	AC k=4	AC k=5
TASI	0.1019*	0.0373	0.0195	-0.0058	0.0319
Subindex 1	0.1187*	0.0402*	0.0389	-0.0116	0.0336
Subindex 2	0.0710*	0.0540*	0.0211	-0.0004	0.0438*
Subindex 3	0.0978*	0.0311	0.0511*	0.0218	-0.0019
Subindex 4	0.0779*	0.0105	0.0141	0.0356	0.0272
Subindex 5	0.1177*	0.0193	0.0438*	0.0004	0.0314
Subindex 6	0.0926*	0.0214	-0.0141	-0.0202	0.0022
Subindex 7	0.0881*	0.0147	-0.0239	0.0082	-0.0082
Subindex 8	0.1366*	0.0432*	0.0154	-0.0217	0.0270
Subindex 9	0.0850*	-0.0006	0.0257	0.0055	0.0127
Subindex 10	0.0716*	0.0354	-0.0315	0.0092	0.0195
Subindex 11	0.1016*	0.0259	-0.0136	0.0053	-0.0184
Subindex 12	-0.1074*	0.0313	-0.0213	0.0285	0.0173
Subindex 13	0.1653*	0.0788*	0.0586*	0.0222	-0.0088
Subindex 14	0.0645*	-0.0196	-0.0283	-0.0042	0.0296
Subindex 15	0.0970*	0.0175	-0.0174	-0.0157	-0.0153

* Indicates the rejection of no autocorrelation at a 5% level of significance for the autocorrelation value outside of the upper and lower confidence bounds of ± 0.0399.

Table 7: Autocorrelation function test

Ljung-Box Q test (daily 06.01.2007-05.01.2017)

	LBQ test				
Number of lags, k	p-value @ k=1	p-value @ k=2	p-value @ k=3	p-value @ k=4	p-value @ k=5
TASI	0.0000*	0.0000*	0.0000*	0.0000*	0.0000*
Subindex 1	0.0000*	0.0000*	0.0000*	0.0000*	0.0000*
Subindex 2	0.0004*	0.0000*	0.0001*	0.0003*	0.0001*
Subindex 3	0.0000*	0.0000*	0.0000*	0.0000*	0.0000*
Subindex 4	0.0001*	0.0004*	0.0011*	0.0007*	0.0008*
Subindex 5	0.0000*	0.0000*	0.0000*	0.0000*	0.0000*
Subindex 6	0.0000*	0.0000*	0.0000*	0.0001*	0.0002*
Subindex 7	0.0000*	0.0000*	0.0001*	0.0002*	0.0006*
Subindex 8	0.0000*	0.0000*	0.0000*	0.0000*	0.0000*
Subindex 9	0.0000*	0.0001*	0.0002*	0.0005*	0.0011*
Subindex 10	0.0003*	0.0003*	0.0003*	0.0009*	0.0014*
Subindex 11	0.0000*	0.0000*	0.0000*	0.0000*	0.0000*
Subindex 12	0.0000*	0.0000*	0.0000*	0.0000*	0.0000*
Subindex 13	0.0000*	0.0000*	0.0000*	0.0000*	0.0000*
Subindex 14	0.0012*	0.0033*	0.0038*	0.0092*	0.0078*
Subindex 15	0.0000*	0.0000*	0.0000*	0.0000*	0.0001*

* Indicates the rejection of the null hypothesis of no autocorrelation at a 5% level of significance for p-values below 0.05.

Table 8: Ljung-Box Q test

2.2.2.4 Variance ratio test

The variance ratio test is based on the fact that if a time series of stock prices follows a random walk, the homoskedastic and heteroskedastic increments are serially uncorrelated and the variance of those increments must be a linear function of the time intervals (Lo & MacKinlay, 1999). The core element of the variance ratio test according to Lo and MacKinlay (1988) is its asymptotic distribution derived under the assumption that k is fixed and T goes to infinity.

The null hypothesis of the variance ratio test is defined as (Cecchetti & Lam, 1994):

$$H_0 = \text{no serial correlation}$$

whereas the alternative hypothesis is given by:

$$H_1 = \text{serial correlation}$$

The variance ratio is the variance of the kth difference of a time series divided by k times the variance of its first difference (Cochrane, 1988):

$$VR(k) = \frac{\sigma^2(k)}{\sigma^2(1)} \tag{13}$$

where (Lo & MacKinlay, 1999):

$$\sigma^2(k) = \frac{1}{m}\sum_{t=k}^{T}\left(r_t - r_{t-k} - q\bar{\mu}\right)^2 \tag{14}$$

and:

$$\sigma^2(1) = \frac{1}{T-1}\sum_{t=1}^{T}\left(r_t - r_{t-k} - \bar{\mu}\right)^2 \tag{15}$$

with:

$$m = k(T-k+1)\left(1-\frac{k}{T}\right) \tag{16}$$

Assuming homoskedastic increments, the test statistic is given by (Lo & MacKinlay, 1988):

$$Z(k) = \frac{VR(k)-1}{\phi(k)^{1/2}} \sim N(0,1) \tag{17}$$

with an asymptotic variance $\phi(k)$ of:

$$\phi(k) = \frac{2(2k-1)(k-1)}{3kT} \tag{18}$$

Assuming heteroskedastic increments, the test statistic is given by (Lo & MacKinlay, 1988):

$$Z^*(k) = \frac{VR(k)-1}{\phi^*(k)^{1/2}} \sim N(0,1) \tag{19}$$

with an asymptotic variance $\phi^*(k)$ of:

$$\phi^*(k) = \sum_{j=1}^{k-1} \left(\frac{2(k-j)}{k} \right)^2 \delta(j) \tag{20}$$

and $\delta(j)$ is given by:

$$\delta(j) = \frac{\sum_{t=j+1}^{T} \left(r_t - \bar{\mu}\right)^2 \left(r_{t-j} - \bar{\mu}\right)^2}{(\sum_{t=1}^{T}(r_t - \bar{\mu})^2)^2} \tag{21}$$

The null hypothesis H_0 is rejected at the 5% level of significance if the test statistics lie outside the interval from $\pm z_{.025}$ (Campbell, Lo, & MacKinlay, 1997). The null hypothesis cannot be rejected for $VR(k) = 1$ for all ks, which means that the time series follows a random walk. According to Campbell, Lo, and MacKinlay (1997), k is selected as $2, 4, 8$, and 16. Cases where the random walk hypothesis is rejected and $VR(k) > 1$ returns are positively serially correlated and cases where the random walk hypothesis is rejected and $VR(k) < 1$ returns are negatively serially correlated describe a mean-reverting process in time series (Fama & French, 1988). Table 9 below shows the results of the variance ration test for the continuous daily dataset.

Variance ratio test (daily 06.01.2007-05.01.2017)

	VR test			
Number of lags, k	k=2	k=4	k=8	k=16
TASI				
VR(k)	1.1028	1.2021	1.2553	1.3041
Z(k)	5.1491*	5.4103*	4.3181*	3.4512*
Z*(k)	2.7179*	2.7463*	2.2250*	1.8474
Subindex 1				
VR(k)	1.1193	1.2390	1.2899	1.3511
Z(k)	5.9762*	6.3990*	4.9034*	3.9845*
Z*(k)	3.1056*	3.3561*	2.6883*	2.3069*
Subindex 2				
VR(k)	1.0719	1.1733	1.2617	1.0719
Z(k)	3.5996*	4.6393*	4.4263*	3.8855*

Variance ratio test (daily 06.01.2007-05.01.2017)

	VR test			
Number of lags, k	k=2	k=4	k=8	k=16
Z*(k)	2.1478*	2.5793*	2.4312*	2.1744*
Subindex 3				
VR(k)	1.0987	1.2063	1.3157	1.3370
Z(k)	4.9419*	5.5218*	5.3400*	3.8252*
Z*(k)	2.5925*	2.9443*	2.9540*	2.1915*
Subindex 4				
VR(k)	1.0792	1.1376	1.1899	1.1383
Z(k)	3.9652*	3.6831*	3.2130*	1.5702
Z*(k)	2.0930*	1.8946	1.6779	0.8489
Subindex 5				
VR(k)	1.1186	1.2205	1.3308	1.4978
Z(k)	5.9377*	5.9031*	5.5958*	5.6497*
Z*(k)	3.8329*	3.8173*	3.7260*	3.9476*
Subindex 6				
VR(k)	1.0931	1.1549	1.1513	1.1222
Z(k)	4.6636*	4.1475*	2.5595*	1.3866
Z*(k)	2.5370*	2.3022*	1.4753	0.8327
Subindex 7				
VR(k)	1.0891	1.1372	1.1342	1.1939
Z(k)	4.4608*	3.6721*	2.2709*	2.2010*
Z*(k)	2.5032*	2.0441*	1.3027	1.3342
Subindex 8				
VR(k)	1.1375	1.1281	1.2849	1.3080
Z(k)	6.8876*	6.9081*	4.8196*	3.4957*
Z*(k)	3.5498*	3.4108*	2.4020*	1.8225
Subindex 9				
VR(k)	1.0863	1.1432	1.1730	1.1735
Z(k)	4.3201*	3.8335*	2.9263*	1.9692*
Z*(k)	2.5607*	2.2561*	1.7431	1.2145
Subindex 10				
VR(k)	1.0724	1.1293	1.1449	1.1723
Z(k)	3.6251*	3.4614*	2.4505*	1.9559
Z*(k)	2.0088*	1.8339	1.3240	1.1119
Subindex 11				
VR(k)	1.1027	1.1744	1.1426	0.9945
Z(k)	5.1415*	4.6687*	2.4130*	-0.0619
Z*(k)	2.5538*	2.3646*	1.2800	-0.0344
Subindex 12				

Variance ratio test (daily 06.01.2007-05.01.2017)				
	VR test			
Number of lags, k	k=2	k=4	k=8	k=16
VR(k)	0.8930	0.8614	0.8633	0.8477
Z(k)	-5.3580*	-3.711*	-2.3130*	-1.7286
Z*(k)	-2.8716*	-2.1054*	-1.4177	-1.1286
Subindex 13				
VR(k)	1.1665	1.3599	1.4885	1.5608
Z(k)	8.3386*	9.6342*	8.2635*	6.3651*
Z*(k)	4.4305*	5.3913*	4.9992*	4.0577*
Subindex 14				
VR(k)	1.0656	1.0657	1.0609	1.1027
Z(k)	3.2837*	1.7581	1.0305	1.1655
Z*(k)	1.8283	0.9714	0.5863	0.6929
Subindex 15				
VR(k)	1.0975	1.1559	1.1499	1.1658
Z(k)	4.8841*	4.1736*	2.5359*	1.8817
Z*(k)	3.2521*	2.7262*	1.6949	1.3012

* Indicates the rejection of no serial correlation at a 5% level of significance for Z and Z* statistic outside of the interval ±1.96.

Table 9: Variance ratio test

2.2.2.5 Pearson product-moment correlation coefficient for serial correlation and Spearman rank correlation

The Pearson product-moment correlation coefficient is a measure of the strength and direction of a linear association between two variables with a normal distribution (Pearson, 1920; Ahlgren, Jarneving, & Rousseau, 2003). In addition, the Spearman rank correlation coefficient is a nonparametric rank statistic proposed as a measure of the strength and direction of the association between two variables (Hauke & Kossowski, 2011). For both tests, the strength of the relationship between the two variables is indicated by the correlation coefficient r in the interval from -1 (perfectly negatively correlated) to 0 (not correlated) to +1 (perfectly positively correlated), but actually measured by the coefficient of determination r^2 (Ahlgren, Jarneving,

& Rousseau, 2003), while the significance of the relationship is given by p (Rodgers & Nicewander, 1988).

The null hypothesis of the Pearson and the Spearman tests for serial correlation is defined as (Ball & Kothari, 1989):

$$H_o = \text{no serial correlation}$$

whereas the alternative hypothesis is given by:

$$H_1 = \text{serial correlation}$$

The Pearson product-moment correlation coefficient is defined as (Croux & Dehon, 2010):

$$r_P = \frac{\sum_{i=1}^{n} (x_i - \bar{x}) \left(y_i - \bar{y}\right)}{\sqrt{\sum_{i=1}^{n} (x_i - \bar{x})^2 \sum_{i=1}^{n} \left(y_i - \bar{y}\right)^2}} \tag{22}$$

where x is defined as the time series and y as the one-lagged period of x.

The Spearman rank correlation coefficient is defined as the Pearson correlation coefficient between ranked variables (Jerome & Well, 2003) and is given by (Spearman, 1904):

$$r_S = \frac{\sum_{i=1}^{n} \left(rg\,(x_i) - \overline{rg}_x\right) \left(rg\left(y_i\right) - \overline{rg}_y\right)}{\sqrt{\sum_{i=1}^{n} \left(rg\,(x_i) - \overline{rg}_x\right)^2 \sum_{i=1}^{n} \left(rg\left(y_i\right) - \overline{rg}_y\right)^2}} \tag{23}$$

where rg defines the ranks and $\overline{rg}$ is the mean of rg. The Spearman rank correlation coefficient is approximated via (Fieller, Hartley, & Pearson, 1957):

$$r_S = \frac{1 - 6S_S}{\left(n^3 - n\right)} \tag{24}$$

with S_S given as:

$$S_S = \sum_{i=1}^{n} \left(rg\,(x_i) - rg\left(y_i\right)\right)^2 \tag{25}$$

In accordance with Cohen (1988), correlation coefficients r_P and r_S on the order of 0.1 are considered small while those around 0.3 are medium and those around 0.5 are large in terms of magnitude of effect size for both positive and negative values. From the permutation argument (Kendall & Stuart, 1973), the relationship between the two variables p is determined as significant for $p < 0.05$ or via the Student's t distribution as follows (Gosset, 1908):

$$t = r\sqrt{\frac{n-2}{1-r^2}} \tag{26}$$

at the 5% level of significance for the two-tailed test. For cases where the correlation coefficients significantly deviate from zero, the null hypothesis H_0 must be rejected, which is a sign of possible market inefficiencies. Tables 10 and 11 below show the results of the Pearson and Spearman tests for the continuous daily dataset.

Pearson product-moment correlation coefficient test (daily 06.01.2007-05.01.2017)

	PCC test	
	Pearson's linear correlation coefficient	p-value
TASI	0.1020	0.0000*
Subindex 1	0.1188	0.0000*
Subindex 2	0.0710	0.0004*
Subindex 3	0.0978	0.0000*
Subindex 4	0.0780	0.0001*
Subindex 5	0.1177	0.0000*
Subindex 6	0.0926	0.0000*
Subindex 7	0.0882	0.0000*
Subindex 8	0.1367	0.0000*
Subindex 9	0.0851	0.0000*
Subindex 10	0.0717	0.0003*
Subindex 11	0.1017	0.0000*
Subindex 12	0.1075	0.0000*
Subindex 13	0.1653	0.0000*
Subindex 14	0.0646	0.0012*
Subindex 15	0.0970	0.0000*

* Indicates the rejection of the null hypothesis of no serial correlation at a 1% level of significance for p-values below 0.01.

Table 10: Pearson product-moment correlation coefficient test

Spearman rank correlation test (daily 06.01.2007-05.01.2017)		
	SRC test	
	Spearman's rho	p-value
TASI	0.1049	0.0000*
Subindex 1	0.1482	0.0000*
Subindex 2	0.0597	0.0028*
Subindex 3	0.1199	0.0000*
Subindex 4	0.0831	0.0000*
Subindex 5	0.1220	0.0000*
Subindex 6	0.0957	0.0000*
Subindex 7	0.0524	0.0087*
Subindex 8	0.1207	0.0000*
Subindex 9	0.0402	0.0439
Subindex 10	0.0612	0.0022*
Subindex 11	0.0967	0.0000*
Subindex 12	-0.0635	0.0015*
Subindex 13	0.0520	0.0092*
Subindex 14	0.0512	0.0103
Subindex 15	0.0664	0.0009*

* Indicates the rejection of the null hypothesis of no serial correlation at a 1% level of significance for p-values below 0.01.

Table 11: Spearman rank correlation test

2.2.2.6 Wald-Wolfowitz runs test

The approach of testing serial correlation via runs tests was introduced by Fama in 1965 to indicate dependence in successive price changes. A run is defined as a series of price changes of the same sign (Fama, 1965). The applied method for the runs test is the Wald-Wolfowitz runs test, a nonparametric test used to determine for independence between successive series without requiring normality of the distribution (Bradley, 1968). The null hypothesis of the Wald-Wolfowitz runs test is defined as:

$$H_0 = \text{no serial correlation}$$

whereas the alternative hypothesis is given by:

$$H_1 = \text{serial correlation}$$

at the 5% level of significance α based on the approximation of the two-tailed standard normal distribution Z for a large number of observations defining the rejection of H_o as:

$$|Z| = Z_{1-\alpha/2} \tag{27}$$

According to Wald and Wolfowitz (1940), Z is calculated as:

$$Z = \frac{R - E_R}{\sigma_R} \tag{28}$$

with given number of runs R as well as expected number of runs E_R and the variance of the number of runs σ_R defined as:

$$E_R = 1 + \frac{2ud}{u + d} \tag{29}$$

$$\sigma_R = \sqrt{\frac{2ud(2ud - u - d)}{(u + d)^2(u + d + 1)}} \tag{30}$$

where u and d are the values above and below the median of the time series. Table 12 below provides the results of the Wald-Wolfowitz runs test for the continuous daily dataset.

Wald-Wolfowitz runs test (daily 06.01.2007-05.01.2017)

	WWR test				
	# of runs	# of values >the mean	# of values <the mean	z-statistic	p-value
TASI	1154	1386	1123	-3.5218	0.0004*
Subindex 1	1129	1258	1251	-5.0316	0.0000*
Subindex 2	1200	1306	1203	-2.1156	0.0344*
Subindex 3	1171	1283	1226	-3.3305	0.0009*
Subindex 4	1188	1303	1206	-2.6047	0.0092*
Subindex 5	1152	1336	1173	-3.9185	0.0001*
Subindex 6	1197	1316	1193	-2.2012	0.0277*
Subindex 7	1201	1259	1250	-2.1559	0.0311*
Subindex 8	1118	1421	1088	-4.6710	0.0000*
Subindex 9	1229	1343	1166	-0.7930	0.4278
Subindex 10	1180	1326	1183	-2.8417	0.0045*
Subindex 11	1164	1312	1197	-3.5364	0.0004*
Subindex 12	1289	1202	1307	1.4081	0.1591
Subindex 13	1233	1213	1296	-0.8247	0.4096
Subindex 14	1199	1280	1229	-2.2166	0.0266*
Subindex 15	1198	1251	1258	-2.2760	0.0228*

* Indicates the rejection of the null hypothesis of no serial correlation at a 5% level of significance for p-values below 0.05.

Table 12: Wald-Wolfowitz runs test

2.2.2.7 Runs test via Shannon entropy

Based on Clausius (1857) on the concept of entropy as a measure of the amount of energy in a thermodynamic system, Shannon (1948) considers entropy a useful measure of uncertainty in the context of communication theory. Following Molgedey and Ebeling (2000) and Risso (2008), Shannon entropy is applied as a method of measuring information efficiency in stock markets by investigating the possibility of finding deterministic chaos in the financial markets, or at least fractal Brownian motion. To conduct the calculation according to Shannon entropy, the time series data are transformed into a symbolic time series, since symbolic analysis is a powerful tool in detecting the very dynamic of highly noisy time series, as are our asset returns (Risso, 2007). The transformation is executed by replacing all values below the mean of the time series by 0 while all values above the mean are replaced by 1. The calculation of normalized Shannon entropy is given by (Risso, 2009):

$$H = \left(\frac{1}{\log_2(n)}\right) \sum p_i \log_2 p_i \qquad (31)$$

where n is defined as the total number of sequences, p is the probability of returns below the mean, and $(1 - p)$ is the probability of returns above the mean. As the equation is concave, the maximum value for entropy of 1 is obtained for $(p = 0.5)$ when the process is completely random, and the minimum value of 0 is obtained when one of the events is absolutely certain ($p = 0$ or $p = 1$). Application of Shannon entropy recovers the information, detecting the formation of patterns in the time series and transforming the measure of uncertainty into a measure of weak-form market efficiency. The new enhancement of this method affords the possibility of studying the evolution of the degree of efficiency over time and detecting long-term correlations like those found in fractional Brownian motion (Risso, 2008). Therefore, a time window of 100 observations is selected and moved across the time series to capture the locality of events in time with Shannon entropy calculated at each data point of the time series over the entire dataset.

The null hypothesis of Shannon entropy is defined as:

$$H_0 = \text{no serial correlation}$$

whereas the alternative hypothesis is given by:

$$H_1 = \text{serial correlation}$$

The null hypothesis for the investigated time series is rejected when either the mean or the minimum or both the mean and the minimum of H lie two standard deviations below the average reference values originating from multiple time series of the same length and consisting of independent and identically distributed random variables. Table

13 below presents the results of the Shannon entropy test for the continuous daily dataset.

Shannon entropy test (daily 06.01.2007-05.01.2017)

	SE test	
	SE mean	SE min
TASI	0.9816*	0.8932*
Subindex 1	0.9926	0.9580
Subindex 2	0.9912*	0.9341
Subindex 3	0.9910*	0.9248*
Subindex 4	0.9900*	0.8932*
Subindex 5	0.9860*	0.9149*
Subindex 6	0.9894*	0.9341
Subindex 7	0.9892*	0.8932*
Subindex 8	0.9774*	0.8415*
Subindex 9	0.9893*	0.8813*
Subindex 10	0.9922	0.9341
Subindex 11	0.9910*	0.9149*
Subindex 12	0.9904*	0.9341
Subindex 13	0.9919	0.9341
Subindex 14	0.9906*	0.9248*
Subindex 15	0.9936	0.9248*

* Indicates the rejection of the null hypothesis of no serial correlation at a 5% level of significance for values below the critical values of 0.9914 (SE mean) and 0.9293 (SE min).

Table 13: Shannon entropy test

2.2.2.8 Rescaled range statistic via Hurst exponent and Lo modified

To detect long-range dependence in economic time series, Mandelbrot (1972) proposed using the range over standard deviation, or R/S statistic, which is a simple generalization of a statistic developed by the English hydrologist Harold Edwin Hurst (1951) in his studies of river discharges, showing persistence in autocorrelations for the first time. The Hurst exponent is used to describe the weak stationary process, which has a long-term memory.

The R/S statistic is given by the range of the partial sums of deviations of a time series from its mean, rescaled by its standard deviation (Lo & MacKinlay, 1999):

$$Q_n = \frac{1}{s_n}\left(\max_{1\leq k\leq n}\sum_{j=1}^{k}\left(x_j - \bar{x}_n\right) - \min_{1\leq k\leq n}\sum_{j=1}^{k}\left(x_j - \bar{x}_n\right)\right) \tag{32}$$

where s_n is the maximum likelihood estimator of the standard deviation of x:

$$\mathrm{s_n} = \sqrt{\frac{1}{\mathrm{n}}\sum_{\mathrm{j=1}}^{\mathrm{n}}\left(\mathrm{x_j} - \bar{\mathrm{x}}_\mathrm{n}\right)^2} \tag{33}$$

The Hurst exponent is expressed as (Lo & MacKinlay, 1999):

$$H = \frac{\log\left(Q_n\right)}{\log(n)} \tag{34}$$

Although the R/S statistic has been refined over time by Mandelbrot (1979), in several important ways it has the shortcoming of its sensitivity to short-range dependency (Campbell, Lo, & MacKinlay, 1997). To distinguish between long- and short-range dependence, the R/S statistic was modified by Lo (1991) accounting for the presence of higher frequency autocorrelation by applying a Newey-West correction with the usage of the Bartlett window to derive a consistent estimate of the long-range variance of time series, replacing s_n with $\hat{\sigma}_n^2$.

$$\hat{\sigma}_n^2 = \frac{1}{n}\sum_{j=1}^{n}\left(x_j - \bar{x}_n\right)^2 + \frac{2}{n}\sum_{j=1}^{q}\left(1 - \frac{j}{q+1}\right)\left(\sum_{i=j+1}^{n}\left(x_i - \bar{x}_n\right)\left(x_{i-j} - \bar{x}_n\right)\right) \tag{35}$$

The test statistic $V_n(q)$ is given by (Lo, 1991) as:

$$\frac{Q_n}{\sqrt{n}} \tag{36}$$

and is computed with q chosen by the Andrews (1991) data-dependent formula:

$$q = \left(\frac{3n}{2}\right)^{1/3} * \left(\frac{2\hat{p}}{1-\hat{p}^2}\right)^{2/3} \tag{37}$$

where $\hat{p}$ is the estimated first-order autocorrelation coefficient of the data.

The null hypothesis of the long-range dependency test via the R/S statistic is defined for both tests as (Jin, 2016):

$$H_o = \text{no long range dependency}$$

whereas the alternative hypothesis is given by:

$$H_1 = \text{long range dependency}$$

A Hurst exponent of 0.5 implies an independent time series following the non-deterministic process of a Brownian motion, while a Hurst exponent less than 0.5 indicates anti-persistent behavior, and a Hurst exponent greater than 0.5 indicates persistent behavior (Couillard & Davison, 2005). At the 5% level of significance, the null hypothesis of the R/S Lo modified test is rejected when the test statistic $V_n(q)$ lies outside the interval from 0.809 to 1.862 (Lo, 1991). Tables 14 and 15 below provide the results of the R/S statistic tests for the continuous daily dataset.

Rescaled range statistic test (Hurst exponent) (daily 06.01.2007-05.01.2017)	
	HE test
	HE
TASI	0.5706
Subindex 1	0.5361
Subindex 2	0.6002*
Subindex 3	0.6018*
Subindex 4	0.5761
Subindex 5	0.5343
Subindex 6	0.5245
Subindex 7	0.5148
Subindex 8	0.5487
Subindex 9	0.5506
Subindex 10	0.4801
Subindex 11	0.5230
Subindex 12	0.4784
Subindex 13	0.5767
Subindex 14	0.5364
Subindex 15	0.5595

* Indicates the rejection of the null hypothesis of no long range dependency at a 5% level of significance for values outside of the interval from 0.3976 to 0.5969.

Table 14: Rescaled range statistic test (Hurst exponent)

Rescaled range statistic test (Lo modified) (daily 06.01.2007-05.01.2017)	
	LM test
	LM
TASI	1.2961
Subindex 1	1.3493
Subindex 2	1.4778
Subindex 3	1.9472*
Subindex 4	1.7797
Subindex 5	1.5654
Subindex 6	1.5805
Subindex 7	1.4558
Subindex 8	1.1587
Subindex 9	1.4404
Subindex 10	1.1283
Subindex 11	1.3710
Subindex 12	0.8772
Subindex 13	1.6185
Subindex 14	1.4014
Subindex 15	1.5076

* Indicates the rejection of the null hypothesis of no long range dependency at a 5% level of significance for values outside of the interval from 0.809 to 1.862.

Table 15: Rescaled range statistic test (Lo modified)

2.3 Results

The upcoming section describes the aggregated individual test results, which are given below the methodology subsections. An overview of the results of the 12 test methods in Table 16 yields a consistent outcome rejecting the weak-form market efficiency hypothesis for the TASI from 2007 to 2017, with the exception of no evidence for long-range dependency.[1]

1 The first two columns provide the results for stationarity tests, the next eight columns for autocorrelation tests, and the last two columns for long range dependency tests. This order applies for the following seven tables.

Results overview (daily 06.01.2007-05.01.2017)

	Overview											
	ADF test	PP test	DW test	ACF test	LBQ test	PCC test	SRC test	WWR test	SE test	VR test	HE test	LM test
TASI	1	1	1	1	1	1	1	1	1	1	0	0
Subindex 1	1	1	1	1	1	1	1	1	0	1	0	0
Subindex 2	1	1	1	1	1	1	1	1	1	1	1	0
Subindex 3	1	1	1	1	1	1	1	1	1	1	1	1
Subindex 4	1	1	1	1	1	1	1	1	1	1	0	0
Subindex 5	1	1	1	1	1	1	1	1	1	1	0	0
Subindex 6	1	1	1	1	1	1	1	1	1	1	0	0
Subindex 7	1	1	1	1	1	1	1	1	1	1	0	0
Subindex 8	1	1	1	1	1	1	1	1	1	1	0	0
Subindex 9	1	1	1	1	1	1	0	0	1	1	0	0
Subindex 10	1	1	1	1	1	1	1	1	0	1	0	0
Subindex 11	1	1	1	1	1	1	1	1	1	1	0	0
Subindex 12	1	1	1	1	1	1	1	0	1	1	0	0
Subindex 13	1	1	1	1	1	1	1	0	0	1	0	0
Subindex 14	1	1	1	1	1	1	0	1	1	1	0	0
Subindex 15	1	1	1	1	1	1	1	1	1	1	0	0

"1" indicates the rejection of the weak form market efficiency hypothesis.

Table 16: Results overview for continuous daily dataset

Rejecting the weak-form market efficiency hypothesis for the TASI is in accordance with the results of previous research, as shown in the literature review section, but with more recent data and leaving aside the absence of long-range dependency, which is documented by Charfeddine and Khediri (2016) and Sensoy (2013). The results for the subindices reveal a largely similar empirical outcome. A deviation lies in subindex 3, where evidence for long-term dependence is present, while for subindices 9 and 13, only an insignificant minority of test methods reject serial correlation. These outcomes partly contradict the results for the subindices in the current literature, where Budd (2012) finds some evidence for weak-form market efficiency in subindices 1, 5, 6, and 8, and Asiri and Alzeera (2013) find that all subindices other than subindices 1, 5, 8, and 12 meet the properties of weak-form efficiency. Considering the exhaustive set of methods employed, we extend the literature by rejecting weak-form market efficiency for all subindices of the Tadawul in the entire study timeframe, with the Tadawul containing 15 subindices from 2007 to 2017.

In contrast to the daily dataset, the change to weekly data frequency results in a different outcome, failing to achieve frequency-independent robust results as shown in Table 17.

Results overview (weekly 06.01.2007-05.01.2017)

	Overview											
	ADF test	PP test	DW test	ACF test	LBQ test	PCC test	SRC test	WWR test	SE test	VR test	HE test	LM test
TASI	1	1	0	0	0	0	0	0	1	0	0	0
Subindex 1	1	1	0	0	0	0	0	0	0	0	0	0
Subindex 2	1	1	1	1	1	1	1	1	0	1	0	0
Subindex 3	1	1	0	1	1	0	0	0	0	0	1	0
Subindex 4	1	1	0	0	0	0	0	0	1	0	1	0
Subindex 5	1	1	0	0	1	0	0	1	1	1	0	0
Subindex 6	1	1	0	0	0	0	0	0	1	0	0	0
Subindex 7	1	1	0	0	0	0	0	0	0	0	0	0
Subindex 8	1	1	0	0	0	0	0	1	1	0	0	0
Subindex 9	1	1	0	0	0	0	0	0	1	0	0	0
Subindex 10	1	1	0	0	0	0	0	0	1	0	0	0
Subindex 11	1	1	0	1	1	1	0	0	1	1	0	0
Subindex 12	1	1	0	0	0	0	0	0	0	0	0	0
Subindex 13	1	1	0	1	0	0	0	0	0	0	0	0
Subindex 14	1	1	0	1	1	0	0	0	0	0	0	0
Subindex 15	1	1	0	0	0	0	0	0	1	0	0	0

"1" indicates the rejection of the weak form market efficiency hypothesis.

Table 17: Results overview for continuous weekly dataset

These results align with Bley (2011) in not rejecting the weak-form market efficiency hypothesis of the Tadawul with weekly input data. The influencing factor of changes in data frequency on the outcome of weak-form market efficiency tests is not unexpected, as this outcome has been part of the literature since Lo and MacKinlay (1988).

We find that weak-form market efficiency of the TASI, as well as for its subindices, does not increase over time. However, change in the degree of weak-form market efficiency can be attributed to the five segmented datasets, as shown in Tables 18 to 22 below.

Results overview (daily 06.01.2007-04.01.2009)

	Overview											
	ADF test	PP test	DW test	ACF test	LBQ test	PCC test	SRC test	WWR test	SE test	VR test	HE test	LM test
TASI	1	1	0	1	1	0	0	1	1	1	0	0
Subindex 1	1	1	1	1	1	1	1	0	1	1	0	0
Subindex 2	1	1	1	1	1	0	0	0	1	1	0	1
Subindex 3	1	1	0	0	0	0	0	1	1	0	0	0
Subindex 4	1	1	0	0	0	0	0	0	0	0	0	0
Subindex 5	1	1	1	1	1	1	1	1	1	1	0	1
Subindex 6	1	1	0	1	1	0	1	0	1	1	0	0
Subindex 7	1	1	0	0	1	0	0	0	1	1	0	0
Subindex 8	1	1	1	1	1	1	1	0	1	1	0	0
Subindex 9	1	1	0	1	1	0	0	0	1	1	0	0
Subindex 10	1	1	0	0	1	0	0	0	0	0	0	0
Subindex 11	1	1	0	1	1	0	0	0	1	1	0	0
Subindex 12	1	1	1	1	1	1	1	1	1	1	0	0
Subindex 13	1	1	0	1	0	0	0	0	0	0	0	0
Subindex 14	1	1	0	0	0	0	0	0	1	0	0	0
Subindex 15	1	1	0	0	0	0	0	0	0	0	0	0

"1" indicates the rejection of the weak form market efficiency hypothesis.

Table 18: Results overview for daily dataset first segment

Results overview (daily 05.01.2009-04.01.2011)

	Overview											
	ADF test	PP test	DW test	ACF test	LBQ test	PCC test	SRC test	WWR test	SE test	VR test	HE test	LM test
TASI	1	1	0	1	0	0	0	0	0	0	0	0
Subindex 1	1	1	0	1	1	0	0	0	1	1	0	0
Subindex 2	1	1	0	0	0	0	0	0	0	0	0	0
Subindex 3	1	1	0	0	0	0	0	0	1	0	0	0
Subindex 4	1	1	0	0	0	0	0	0	1	0	0	0
Subindex 5	1	1	0	1	1	1	0	0	1	1	0	0
Subindex 6	1	1	0	0	0	0	0	0	0	0	0	0
Subindex 7	1	1	0	0	0	0	0	0	1	0	0	0
Subindex 8	1	1	0	1	1	0	0	0	1	1	0	0
Subindex 9	1	1	0	0	0	0	0	1	0	0	0	0
Subindex 10	1	1	0	1	1	0	0	0	0	0	0	0
Subindex 11	1	1	0	0	0	0	0	0	0	1	0	0
Subindex 12	1	1	0	1	1	0	0	0	1	0	0	0
Subindex 13	1	1	0	0	0	0	0	0	0	0	0	0
Subindex 14	1	1	0	0	0	0	0	0	0	0	0	0
Subindex 15	1	1	0	0	0	0	0	0	0	0	0	0

"1" indicates the rejection of the weak form market efficiency hypothesis.

Table 19: Results overview for daily dataset second segment

Results overview (daily 05.01.2011-09.01.2013)

	Overview											
	ADF test	PP test	DW test	ACF test	LBQ test	PCC test	SRC test	WWR test	SE test	VR test	HE test	LM test
TASI	1	1	0	0	0	0	1	1	1	0	0	0
Subindex 1	1	1	0	0	0	0	1	1	0	1	0	0
Subindex 2	1	1	0	0	0	0	0	1	0	0	0	0
Subindex 3	1	1	1	1	1	1	1	0	1	1	0	0
Subindex 4	1	1	0	1	1	0	0	0	0	0	0	0
Subindex 5	1	1	0	1	0	0	0	1	0	0	0	0
Subindex 6	1	1	0	1	0	0	0	0	0	0	0	0
Subindex 7	1	1	0	1	1	0	1	1	1	1	0	0
Subindex 8	1	1	0	1	1	0	1	1	1	1	0	0
Subindex 9	1	1	0	0	0	0	0	0	1	0	0	0
Subindex 10	1	1	0	0	0	0	1	1	0	0	0	0
Subindex 11	1	1	0	0	0	0	0	0	1	0	0	0
Subindex 12	1	1	0	0	0	0	0	0	0	0	0	0
Subindex 13	1	1	0	0	0	0	0	0	0	0	0	0
Subindex 14	1	1	0	0	0	0	1	0	1	1	0	0
Subindex 15	1	1	0	0	0	0	0	0	1	0	0	0

"1" indicates the rejection of the weak form market efficiency hypothesis.

Table 20: Results overview for daily dataset third segment

Results overview (daily 12.01.2013-15.01.2015)

	Overview											
	ADF test	PP test	DW test	ACF test	LBQ test	PCC test	SRC test	WWR test	SE test	VR test	HE test	LM test
TASI	1	1	1	1	1	1	1	1	1	1	0	0
Subindex 1	1	1	1	1	1	1	1	1	0	1	0	0
Subindex 2	1	1	1	1	1	1	1	0	1	1	0	1
Subindex 3	1	1	1	1	1	0	1	0	0	1	0	0
Subindex 4	1	1	1	1	1	1	1	1	0	1	0	0
Subindex 5	1	1	1	1	1	1	1	1	0	1	0	0
Subindex 6	1	1	1	1	1	1	0	0	0	1	0	1
Subindex 7	1	1	1	1	1	0	0	0	0	1	0	0
Subindex 8	1	1	1	1	1	1	1	1	1	1	0	0
Subindex 9	1	1	1	1	1	1	0	0	0	1	0	0
Subindex 10	1	1	1	1	1	1	1	0	1	1	0	0
Subindex 11	1	1	0	1	1	0	1	1	0	1	0	0
Subindex 12	1	1	0	1	1	0	0	0	1	1	0	0
Subindex 13	1	1	1	1	1	1	1	1	1	1	1	1
Subindex 14	1	1	1	1	1	1	1	1	0	1	0	0
Subindex 15	1	1	1	1	1	1	1	0	0	1	0	0

”1” indicates the rejection of the weak form market efficiency hypothesis.

Table 21: Results overview for daily dataset fourth segment

Results overview (daily 18.01.2015-05.01.2017)

	Overview											
	ADF test	PP test	DW test	ACF test	LBQ test	PCC test	SRC test	WWR test	SE test	VR test	HE test	LM test
TASI	1	1	0	1	1	0	1	0	0	1	0	0
Subindex 1	1	1	0	1	1	0	1	0	0	1	0	0
Subindex 2	1	1	0	1	0	0	0	0	1	1	0	0
Subindex 3	1	1	1	1	1	1	1	1	0	1	0	0
Subindex 4	1	1	1	1	1	1	1	1	1	1	0	0
Subindex 5	1	1	0	1	1	0	0	0	1	1	0	0
Subindex 6	1	1	1	1	1	1	0	0	0	1	0	0
Subindex 7	1	1	0	1	1	0	0	1	1	1	0	0
Subindex 8	1	1	1	1	1	1	1	0	1	1	0	0
Subindex 9	1	1	0	1	1	0	0	0	1	1	0	0
Subindex 10	1	1	0	0	0	0	0	1	1	0	0	0
Subindex 11	1	1	1	1	1	1	1	1	0	1	0	0
Subindex 12	1	1	0	0	0	0	0	0	1	0	0	0
Subindex 13	1	1	1	1	1	1	1	0	1	1	1	0
Subindex 14	1	1	0	0	0	0	0	1	1	1	1	0
Subindex 15	1	1	1	1	1	1	0	0	0	1	0	0

"1" indicates the rejection of the weak form market efficiency hypothesis.

Table 22: Results overview for daily dataset fifth segment

The efficiency of the TASI graduates upward from some degree of efficiency in the first segment to greater efficiency in the second segment and moves over some degree of efficiency in the third segment to inefficiency in the fourth segment, and again to some degree of efficiency in the fifth segment. In addition, Shannon entropy confirms these results and visualizes clusters of reduced efficiency in Figure 1 with peaks around the turn of the year 2011/2012, and to a greater extent, 2013/2014.

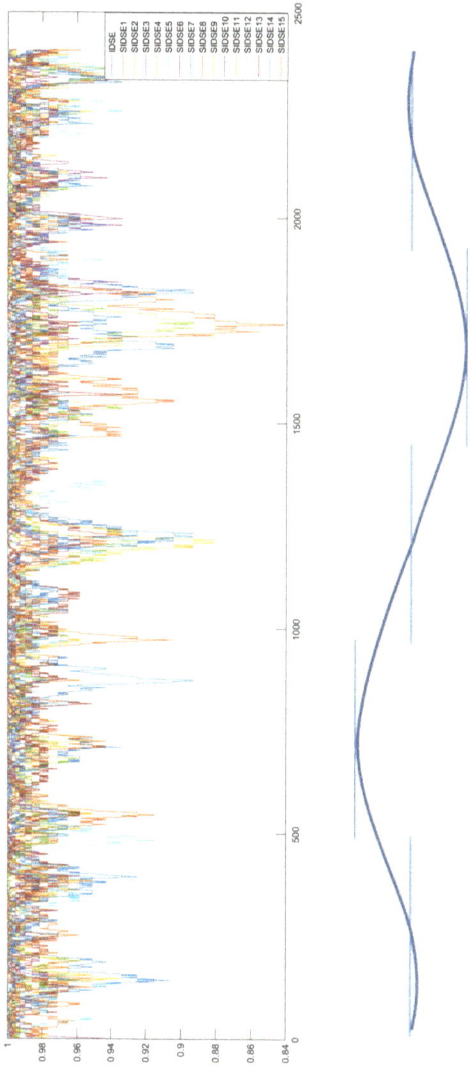

Figure 1: Shannon entropy and degree of efficiency

These outcomes contradict intuition together with logical reasoning, as they provide empirical evidence that the TASI improves in terms of efficiency in the second segment during the time of the financial crisis, and declines in efficiency in the fourth segment during a period of recovery from the financial crisis. However, at least for the first three segments, these results are backed by Arshad et al. (2016) and Abdmoulah (2010), who show empirically similar outcomes for weak-form market efficiency of the TASI before, during, and after the financial crisis. The change in the degrees of weak-form market efficiency of the TASI over the five segmented datasets is reflected by the subindices, with analogous characteristics, although all show a distinct pattern of their own. Looking at the segmented datasets, the results on the subindices in Asiri and Alzeera (2013) and Budd (2012) are moderated, as they do not cover the full period of the Tadawul containing 15 subindices and they originate from a timeframe with a higher degree of weak-form efficiency. A graduating change in the absent long-range dependency is documented neither for the TASI nor for the subindices.

The theoretical and empirical literature provides several reasons for the absence of weak-form market efficiency in the Tadawul that interact and to a great extent interrelate, such as the presence of excessive stock market volatility and information asymmetry as well as weak foreign participation and high concentration in certain subindices, such as banking and petro (Jamaani & Roca, 2015). Further, the mean-reverting tendency of daily stock market returns and the herding behavior of a high proportion of domestic institutional investors (Bley, 2011), as well as the ineffectiveness and implementation difficulties of past reforms (Abdmoulah, 2010), play a significant role in the explanatory value of the results.

2.4 Conclusion

This paper analyzes the weak-form market efficiency hypothesis and the Tadawul with a focus on the Tadawul subindices covering the largest possible time period, that is, 15 subindices from 2007 to 2017. We show that the TASI and all subindices are not weak-form market efficient, but neither do they exhibit long-range dependency. Further, an enhancement of the degree of efficiency could not be documented over the study period. For investors, the rejection of the weak-form market efficiency hypothesis of the TASI and all its 15 subindices provides an opportunity to predict future prices and generate abnormal returns on a systematic and continuous basis by applying mechanical trading rules (Asiri & Alzeera, 2013; Bley, 2011; Jensen, 1978), as future successive price changes can be predicted from past price changes (Jamaani & Roca, 2015), while remaining aware of the potential threat from those inefficiencies. Due to matching results on the level of the subindices, this possibility also applies to investors with a sector or industry focus in the structuring of coherent trading portfolios (Al Janabi, Hatemi-J, & Irandoust, 2010). For policy makers, these results should enhance endeavors toward market efficiency by overcoming information asymmetry and promoting growth apart from the oil and banking industries, as the outcome shows a discrepancy between the actual efficiency of the Tadawul and long-term growth plans (Jamaani & Roca, 2015). The vehicles and instruments to aid this development include, among others, market liberalization, privatization, diversification of financial services, improvement of the investment climate with widespread institutional trading, and structural reforms to accept foreign stock ownership (Bley, 2011; Abdmoulah, 2010).

This paper is not without limitations. Following Jamaani and Roca (2015) on potential problems resulting from the impact of thin trading for the TASI based on increased trading volumes, together with the results from Al-Ajmi and Kim (2012) and Bley (2011), no attempt is made to correct for thin trading. Although this limitation is valid for the TASI, it is adopted to be plausible also for the subindices, without having empirical evidence in this regard.

Future research should carry out a similar study with a structure of 20 subindices, as currently the required data are not available, resulting in a high degree of divergence in the results of market efficiency testing. This does not allow for meaningful results. In addition, future research should further investigate the possibility of transforming existing market inefficiencies into abnormal returns by treating the subindices as asset classes and applying quantitative techniques of portfolio optimization.

3. How successful are active portfolio investment strategies for the Saudi Stock Exchange?

This paper contributes to the literature in several ways. First, to our best knowledge, no previous research has been conducted on optimal portfolio selection resulting from market inefficiencies of the TASI to generate outperforming portfolios on a systemic basis, apart from initial efforts with niche optimization models (Zakaria & Hashim, 2017; Shalan & Ykhlef, 2015). Second, by adding the dimension of a direct time-related coherence between the different degrees of market efficiency observed and the magnitude of the possible outperformance of quantitative asset allocation strategies, we examine whether the ability to predict future prices from past price changes leading to higher abnormal risk-adjusted returns is aligned with the degree of market efficiency of the TASI in the segmented datasets. This is done via application of a well-balanced, exhaustive, and up-to-date set of quantitative asset allocation strategies for portfolio optimization and measurement techniques for validating and collating potential abnormal risk-adjusted returns, leading to methodological validity, variety, and depth. Similar to papers presented in the literature review on investment strategies we use the rolling window approach for optimal portfolio construction. We find that the inefficiencies of the Tadawul can be transformed into abnormal risk-adjusted returns. Further, direct alignment of the graduating degree of market efficiency and the ability to predict future prices from past price changes could not be confirmed.

3.1 Literature review

Optimal portfolio construction, the process of efficiently attributing weightings to assets, has a long history in academic literature (Maillard, Roncalli, & Teiletche, 2010). Markowitz (1952) laid the foundation for modern portfolio theory, formalizing the problem in a mean-variance framework where a rational investor seeks to maximize expected return for a given volatility level, leading, for example, to minimum variance optimization. Based on the mean-variance framework, Sharpe (1966) developed a measurement to overcome the indifference of mean variance efficient frontier portfolios by comparing their expected return per unit of risk, resulting in the Sharpe ratio optimized tangency portfolio (Stoyanov, Rachev, & Fabozzi, 2007). Aiming to overcome the known negative effects of estimation error and input assumptions within the mean-variance framework (Kolm, Tütüncü, & Fabozzi, 2014; Michaud, 1989), progress was made in the development of estimators such as the Bayes-Stein approach of shrinking the sample mean for a particular asset toward the grand mean, which improved the traditional mean-variance optimization significantly (Jorion, 1986; Jobson & Korkie, 1981). In addition, the shrinkage methodology of Ledoit and Wolf (2003a), which balances the estimation error of the sample covariance matrix and the bias of the structured estimator was made optimal by calibrating the shrinkage covariance matrices via minimization of the expected quadratic loss (DeMiguel, Martin-Utrera, & Nogales, 2013). The naïve investment strategy experienced a renaissance in 2009, triggered by DeMiguel, Garlappi, and Uppal, who stated that neither the portfolios of the mean-variance framework nor its extensions were able to consistently deliver outperforming results compared to the naïve portfolio with the researched datasets (DeMiguel, Garlappi, & Uppal, 2009). This was challenged and partly contradicted by a variety of subsequent research (Duchin & Levy, 2009; Kritzman, Page, & Turkington, 2010; Tu & Zhou, 2011). The literature then entered a period characterized by a strong focus on risk management and risk budgeting within the science of portfolio construction (Roncalli & Weisang, 2016), leading to different approaches to risk-enhanced portfolios, such as equal risk contribution, inverse volatility (Maillard, Roncalli, & Teiletche, 2010), most diversified (Choueifaty, Froidure, & Reynier, 2011), and diversified risk parity (Meucci, Santangelo, & Deguest, 2015).

Acceptance of the weak-form market efficiency hypothesis for a particular market and timeframe signifies the absence of arbitrage opportunity for investors that can be used to make excess abnormal profit based on analysis of past price and return information (Risso, 2008). This leads to the logical implication that inefficient markets are characterized by the ability of active investment strategies to outperform the market as a whole due to distortions in the pricing of capital and risk, inhibiting efficient allocation of capital (Jamaani & Roca, 2015; Malkiel, 2003). Following this logic, the TASI creates an opportunity to forecast future prices and generate abnormal risk-adjusted returns while holding a well-diversified portfolio on a systematic and continuous basis by applying mechanical trading rules (Malhotra, Tandon, & Tandon, 2015; Asiri & Alzeera, 2013; Bley, 2011), as future successive price changes can be predicted from past price changes (Jamaani & Roca, 2015). However, some papers advocate passive investment strategies in all types of investment markets regardless of existing efficiency or degree of development, suggesting insufficient predictability from anomalies and irrationalities in stock markets to outperform a passive portfolio with equivalent risk by taking advantage of exploitable arbitrage opportunities (Malkiel, 2003). This framework builds a foundation to connect the weak-form market efficiency hypothesis, which includes the idea that market prices incorporate all information rationally and instantaneously, with the extensive research on portfolio optimization, in which outperformance relative to a benchmark via a distinct quantitative or qualitative active investment strategy is the natural objective framed by a predefined setup of optional constraints (Maillard, Roncalli, & Teiletche, 2010; Lo, 2004; Moskowitz, 2000).

3.2 Data and methodology

The concepts of portfolio optimization and diversification introduced by Markowitz (1952) have been fundamental in understanding financial markets and financial decision making (Kolm, Tütüncü, & Fabozzi, 2014). A concept with equal influence is the efficient market hypothesis consolidated and promoted by Fama (1970), which contains the idea that market prices incorporate all information rationally and instantaneously (Lo, 2004). According to Malkiel (2003), the most direct and convincing test of market efficiency is the ability of active investment strategies to outperform the market as a whole; this is the objective of portfolio optimization (Moskowitz, 2000). This means that in inefficient markets, the ability of active investment strategies to outperform the benchmark must be provable and measurable. Accordingly, our main research objective H_0 (1) is to investigate whether existing market inefficiency in the Tadawul can be transformed into outperforming active investment strategies by treating the subindices as asset classes to which quantitative techniques of portfolio optimization are applied to benchmark the optimized strategies against the TASI. Further, in accordance with our hypothesis, we investigate whether there is an interrelation between the degrees of efficiency discovered in four consecutive subsets of the dataset of equal length, H_0 (2), as well as between the degrees of the efficiency discovered in different data frequencies, H_0 (3), and the magnitude of the outperformance of active investment strategies.

3.2.1 Data

The input data for the empirical analysis contain the TASI and its 15 subindex datasets in daily and, for robustness reasons, weekly frequency from 06.01.2007 to 05.01.2017 (that is, until reclassification in accordance with the Global Industry Classification Standard; Saudi Stock Exchange, 2017). This amounts to 2509 daily and 499 weekly time-dependent data points, of which the first 20% are used as data pre-flow to calibrate a variance-covariance matrix with a rolling window size of two years. For the active investment strategies, these 15 subindices represent the available investment possibilities, which are prioritized for quantitative optimization. The subindices are used instead of individual shares as they enable composition of a stable and homogeneous dataset. A sectoral overview of the 15 subindices is provided in Table 23 below (Saudi Stock Exchange, 2016).

Tadawul and subindices		
Code	Name	Nomenclature paper
SASEIDX	Tadawul	TASI
SASEBNK	Tadawul All Share Banking Index	Subindex 1
SASEPETR	Tadawul All Share Petro Index	Subindex 2
SASECEM	Tadawul All Share Cement Index	Subindex 3
SASERETL	Tadawul All Share Retail Industries Index	Subindex 4
SASEINS	Tadawul All Share Insurance Index	Subindex 5
SASETEL	Tadawul All Share Telecommunications Index	Subindex 6
SASEREAL	Tadawul All Share Real Estate Development Industries Index	Subindex 7
SASEBULD	Tadawul All Share Building & Construction Index	Subindex 8
SASEMINV	Tadawul All Share Multi-Investment Index	Subindex 9
SASEINDI	Tadawul All Share Industrial Investment Industries Index	Subindex 10
SASEAGRI	Tadawul All Share Agriculture & Food Industries Index	Subindex 11
SASEENER	Tadawul All Share Energy & Utilities Industries Index	Subindex 12
SASEMEDI	Tadawul All Share Media & Publishing Industries Index	Subindex 13
SASETRAN	Tadawul All Share Transport Industries Index	Subindex 14
SASEHOTE	Tadawul All Share Hotel & Tourism Industries Index	Subindex 15

Table 23: Subindex sectoral overview

Further, the dataset in daily frequency is split into four segments containing approximately 502 time-dependent data points. All datasets underlying the empirical analysis consist of analysis of logarithmic asset returns common to most financial time series (Tsay, 2005; Campbell, Lo, & MacKinlay, 1997).

3.2.2 Methodology

To test the possibility of transforming existing market inefficiencies into outperforming active investment strategies within the previously described data selection, first, the portfolios of the quantitative asset allocation strategies that represent a well-balanced, exhaustive, and up-to-date selection are determined based on the 15 subindices of the TASI as the available investment spectrum by treating the subindices as asset classes. Second, these portfolios are benchmarked against the TASI, and potential outperformance is quantified according to a set of measurements that consider mainly return and risk and their combination from different perspectives. For the segmented analysis, the average deviation of the TASI from the asset allocation strategies is calculated for each measurement and for all four daily data segments and set in reference to the degree of discovered market efficiency. The results from the market efficiency hypothesis for the exact same data, including frequency and segmentation, are taken from the first paper.

3.2.2.1 Investment strategies

We construct our portfolio in accordance with DeMiguel, Garlappi, and Uppal (2009), with its strong focus on the naïve investment strategy as well as portfolios of the mean-variance framework, and with Kremer, Talmaciu, and Paterlini (2018), who utilize risk management-orientated portfolio strategies. The subsections below provide the mathematical formulation together with the methodological description of the nine investment strategies.

3.2.2.1.1 Minimum variance optimization

The core of modern portfolio theory is the concept of the efficient frontier and, consequently, efficient frontier portfolios (Markowitz, 1952). The minimum variance portfolio is defined as the specific portfolio on the efficient frontier that contains, compared to all other efficient frontier portfolios, the least expected risk measured by volatility and that is, therefore, independent of any expectations of possible returns (Kan & Zhou, 2006). The target function is defined as:

$$\min_{\omega_i} \rightarrow \omega_i^T \sum\nolimits_i \omega_i \tag{38}$$

Reduction in portfolio risk originates mainly from a highly concentrated allocation to assets with low volatility and not exploiting correlation effects between assets (Maillard, Roncalli, & Teiletche, 2010).

3.2.2.1.2 Sharpe ratio optimization

The Sharpe ratio is defined as the excess return of a portfolio over the risk-free rate divided by its total risk (Kopman & Liu, 2009; Sharpe, 1994):

$$SR_{\omega_i} = \frac{\omega_i^T \mu_i - r_f}{\sqrt{\omega_i^T \sum_i \omega_i}} \tag{39}$$

The result is a mean-variance efficient Markowitz (1952) portfolio that identifies the minimum variance portfolio arising from a linear combination of the given assets and the risk-free asset with zero weight allocated (Fabozzi, Focardi, & Kolm, 2006). When defining the risk-free rate as zero, the result is the tangent portfolio to the efficient frontier passing through the origin (Stoyanov, Rachev, & Fabozzi,

2007). This leads to the following optimization problem:

$$\max_{\omega_i} \rightarrow \frac{\omega_i^T \mu_i}{\sqrt{\omega_i^T \Sigma_i \omega_i}} \tag{40}$$

Transferring the maximization problem according to Stoyanov et al. (2007) into the minimization solution of two equivalent problems, it becomes standard quadratic and, consequently, can be solved as a quadratic programming problem.

3.2.2.1.3 Bayes-Stein optimization

The Bayes-Stein shrinkage portfolio aims to mitigate errors in estimating the expected returns via a convex combination, shrinking the sample mean for the particular asset toward the grand mean $\bar{\mu}$ across all assets (Garlappi, Uppal, & Wang, 2007). This brings in the observation of Stein (1956) that a shrinkage estimator shrinking the sample mean appropriately to a constant can have a smaller expected quadratic loss than the sample mean. Under the Bayesian approach, the estimators of μ and Σ are computed using the predictive distribution of asset returns. This was proposed by Jorion, giving an estimator of μ that is motivated by both a shrinkage consideration and a Bayesian analysis, which is given as follows (Jorion, 1986):

$$\hat{\mu}_i^{BS} = \left(1 - \hat{\varphi}_i\right) \hat{\mu}_i + \hat{\varphi}_i \hat{\mu}_i^{\min} \tag{41}$$

where $0 < \hat{\varphi}_i < 1$ and where $\hat{\varphi}_i$ is the weight given to the shrinking target $\hat{\mu}_i^{\min}$ while $\left(1 - \hat{\varphi}_i\right)$ is the weight on the sample mean (Kan & Zhou, 2006). Jorion's shrinking target is the average excess return on the minimum variance portfolio, which means that the grand mean $\bar{\mu}$ is equal to the mean of the minimum variance portfolio $\mu^{\min}$ (DeMiguel, Garlappi, & Uppal, 2009):

$$\hat{\mu}_i^{\min} \equiv \hat{\mu}_i^T \widehat{\omega}_i^{\min} \tag{42}$$

The shrinkage coefficient $\hat{\varphi}_i$ is defined as (Jorion, 1986)

$$\hat{\varphi}_i = \frac{N+2}{(N+2) + M\left(\hat{\mu}_i - \hat{\mu}_i^{\min}\right)^T \widehat{\Sigma}_i^{-1} \left(\hat{\mu}_i - \hat{\mu}_i^{\min}\right)} \tag{43}$$

This leads to the weight vector for the Bayes-Stein shrinkage:

$$\widehat{\omega}_i^{\mathrm{BS}} = \frac{\left(\widehat{\Sigma}_i^{-BS}\right)^{-1} \hat{\mu}_i^{BS}}{1_N \left(\widehat{\Sigma}_i^{-BS}\right)^{-1} \hat{\mu}_i^{BS}} \tag{44}$$

By logic, the optimal coefficient is increasing in the number of assets N while decreasing in the estimation window length M, as well as decreasing in the dispersion of the sample mean $\hat{\mu}$ from the shrinkage target $\bar{\mu}$ (Kolusheva, 2008).

3.2.2.1.4 Ledoit-Wolf optimization

The shrinkage methodology of Ledoit and Wolf extends the approach of Jorion by improving the estimator of the covariance matrix (Ledoit & Wolf, 2003; Jorion, 1986). This shrinkage estimator is designed to optimally balance the estimation error of the sample covariance matrix and the bias of the structured estimator to construct a portfolio with improved performance in expected utility with the aim of finding a compromise between both components, and is expressed as (Ledoit & Wolf, 2003; Ledoit & Wolf, 2004):

$$\sum\nolimits_{\mathrm{Shrink}} = \delta F + (1-\delta) S \tag{45}$$

where S is the sample covariance matrix of past stock returns; F is a highly structured estimator of the covariance matrix; and $0 \leq \delta \leq 1$ is shrinkage intensity, as it determines the weight of F in the convex linear combination between S and F, minimizing their expected distance according to the quadratic loss function based on the Frobenius norm (Ledoit & Wolf, 2004; Wolf, 2004). Estimator F is determined by the sample constant correlation matrix, where all pairwise covariances are identical (Ledoit & Wolf, 2004) instead of the single factor matrix (Ledoit & Wolf, 2003) and the identity matrix (Ledoit & Wolf, 2004). The optimal shrinkage intensity δ can be written as (Ledoit & Wolf, 2004; Lui, 2014).

$$\delta = \frac{\sum_{i=1}^{M}\sum_{j=1}^{N} \mathrm{Var}\left(s_{ij}\right) - \mathrm{Cov}\left(f_{ij}, s_{ij}\right)}{\sum_{i=1}^{M}\sum_{j=1}^{N} \mathrm{Var}\left(f_{ij} - s_{ij}\right) + \left(\phi_{ij} - \sigma_{ij}\right)^{2}} \tag{46}$$

3.2.2.1.5 Rebalanced equally weighted portfolio

The simplest and most intuitive asset allocation possibility is the naïve or equally weighted strategy. Even so, this strategy involves no optimization or estimation and does not take any input into account; it is an extremely challenging strategy to beat consistently (DeMiguel, Garlappi, & Uppal, 2009). The naïve portfolio rule allocates to each of the N assets available in the investment horizon a weight of $1/N$ (Fugazza, Guidolin, & Nicodano, 2010):

$$\omega_{i,j} = \frac{1}{N} \forall j \tag{47}$$

where rebalancing leads to a fully naïve diversified portfolio in every period and, in consequence, to exploitation of the mean-reverting behavior of assets (Chaudhuri & Wu, 2004). The clearest advantages of the equally weighted portfolio are that it contains the least possible weight concentration in each asset and that it does not depend on predictions (Fugazza, Guidolin, & Nicodano, 2010). However, this strategy ignores the risk from individual assets in terms of volatility and from the combined assets in terms of covariances (Kremer, Talmaciu, & Paterlini, 2018). The diversification effect is, therefore, present only with a larger number of assets that are ideally low-correlated.

3.2.2.1.6 Equal-risk-contribution portfolio

The idea behind the equal-risk-contribution portfolio is to maximize diversification of risk by equalizing the risk contributions from all components of the portfolio (Maillard, Roncalli, & Teiletche, 2010). As a result, components with high volatility or high correlation with other assets are ascribed smaller weights in the portfolio (Leote de Carvalho, Lu, & Moulin, 2012). The solution can be numerically obtained as (Griveau-Billion, Richard, & Roncalli, 2013):

$$\omega^* = \operatorname{argmin} \sum_{i=1}^{M} \sum_{j=1}^{N} \left(\omega_j (\Sigma\omega)_j - \omega_i (\Sigma\omega)_i \right)^2 \tag{48}$$

to minimize the variance of risk contributions (Maillard, Roncalli, & Teiletche, 2010). This strategy constitutes a middle ground between minimum variance optimization and the equally weighted portfolio, overcoming their individual major drawbacks, that is, a possibly high asset concentration in the case of the minimum variance optimization and potentially limited diversification of risks in the case of the equally weighted portfolio (Maillard, Roncalli, & Teiletche, 2010). Further, the equal-risk-contribution portfolio is identical to the minimum variance optimization when the correlation and the Sharpe ratio are equal among all assets (Clarke, De Silva, & Thorley, 2013).

3.2.2.1.7 Most diversified portfolio

The most diversified portfolio was introduced by Choueifaty and Coignard (2008) and is defined as the long-only portfolio that maximizes the diversification ratio:

$$\max DR_{\omega_i} \rightarrow \frac{\sum_{j=1}^{N} \omega_j \sigma_j}{\sqrt{\omega_i^T \sum_i \omega_i}} \tag{49}$$

This is explained in subsection 3.2.2.2.6. Even so, this investment strategy lacks an underlying economic theory or an underlying utility function. Fernholz, Garvy, and Hannon (1998) emphasize that investors benefit from the contribution of the difference between the portfolio-weighted sum of asset variances and the portfolio variances. The two core properties of the most diversified portfolio are: 1) the long-only most diversified portfolio is the long-only portfolio such that the correlation between any other long-only portfolio and itself is greater than or equal to the ratio of their diversification ratios; and 2) any stock not held by the most diversified portfolio is more correlated to the most diversified portfolio than any stock belonging to it that has the same correlation to the most diversified portfolio (Choueifaty, Froidure, & Reynier, 2013). The inherent characteristics of the most diversified portfolio result in two special features. First, if all assets have the same Sharpe ratio, the most diversified portfolio is equivalent to the tangency portfolio. Second, if all assets are identically correlated, the most diversified portfolio is identical to the equal-risk-contribution portfolio (Choueifaty & Coignard, 2008).

3.2.2.1.8 Inverse volatility portfolio

Under the assumption of equal correlation for every pair of components, the asset weightings in the risk-parity portfolio are given by the ratios of the inverse of their volatilities to the harmonic average of the volatilities (Maillard, Roncalli, & Teiletche, 2010). The formula for calculating weightings of this inverse volatility portfolio is given as (Chaves, Hsu, Li, & Shakernia, 2012):

$$\omega_i = \frac{\frac{1}{\sigma_i}}{\sum_{j=1}^{N} \frac{1}{\sigma_j}} \tag{50}$$

with the weightings of the components inversely proportional to their volatility, and the higher the volatility of a component, the lower its weight in this portfolio and vice versa. The key benefit of this strategy is its simplicity, as it minimizes the marginal risk concentration based solely on the volatilities. This also defines its major drawback, as cross correlations between the different assets and the resulting diversification potential are not exploited, in contrast to the equal-risk-contribution portfolio (Chaves, Hsu, Li, & Shakernia, 2011). The differences with the minimum variance optimization are that the weightings of the inverse volatility portfolio are proportional to the inverse volatility, instead of the inverse variance, and that all assets of the investment horizon are included (Clarke, De Silva, & Thorley, 2013).

3.2.2.1.9 Diversified-risk-parity portfolio

Shannon (1948) entropy, which was initially developed to solve communications problems, provides a nonlinear model for quantification of the disorder of a random variable in a system (Yu, Lee, & Chiou, 2014). Alternatively, it can be used to measure the expected information in a probability distribution and can, therefore, be taken as a measurement for the degree of dispersion in the diversification distribution (Bera & Park, 2008). Meucci (2009) proposed the exponential of Shannon entropy to measure the degree of portfolio diversification via the effective number of uncorrelated bets (Bernardi, Leippold, &

Lohre, 2018):

$$N_{Ent} = \exp\left(-\sum_{j=1}^{N} p_j \ln p_j\right) \tag{51}$$

where p_j is calculated via the minimum torsion method from Meucci et al. (2015) and $N_{Ent} = 1$ characterizes a completely concentrated portfolio, while $N_{Ent} = N$ represents the maximum diversification resulting in the equally weighted portfolio (Meucci, 2009). This measurement can be used as an asset allocation strategy to build the diversified risk-parity portfolio by solving the following nonlinear optimization problem (Lohre, Opfer, & Orszäg, 2014):

$$\omega^* = \operatorname{argmax} N_{Ent}(\omega) \tag{52}$$

The difference between the equal-risk-contribution portfolio and the diversified-risk-parity portfolio is based on different risk measures, with the equal-risk-contribution approach aiming to diversify a portfolio according to equal risk contributions, whereas the diversified-risk-parity approach defines a well-diversified portfolio such that the elements p_j of the diversification distribution are uniformly distributed and approximately equal (Maillard, Roncalli, & Teiletche, 2010; Meucci, Santangelo, & Deguest, 2015).

3.2.2.2 Measurements

The ability to transform existing market inefficiencies into outperforming active investment strategies is quantified via comparison of the investment strategies described above with the index benchmark TASI according to the following measurements: return, variance, Sharpe ratio, value at risk, certainty equivalent return, diversification ratio, and turnover rate, allowing for a deep evaluation from different perspectives. Below, we provide the mathematical formulation, explain the measurements in greater detail where required, and conclude with a short overview focusing on explanatory power. The individual result tables and figures are given below each measurement subsection. The aggregated results are provided in the results section.

3.2.2.2.1 Mean return

Return is the ratio of money gained or lost on an investment over a particular period relative to the amount of money invested. Logarithmic or contiguously compounded return is computed via (Campbell, Lo, & MacKinlay, 1997; Markowitz H., 1991):

$$r_i = \log(P_i) - \log(P_{i-1}) \tag{53}$$

The return of a portfolio containing N assets is mathematically expressed as:

$$r_i = \sum_{j=1}^{n} \omega_j^T \times r_j \tag{54}$$

and the arithmetic mean of the contiguously compounded return is defined as:

$$AM(R) = \frac{1}{m} \sum_{i=1}^{m} r_i \tag{55}$$

The above-stated method contains the desired favorable statistical properties and thus contrasts with the stock and market information more common in theoretical models and financial modeling (DeFusco, McLeavey, Pinto, & Runkle, 2007). Table 24 below shows the results of the mean return.

Mean return[2]	daily	weekly	1st segment	2nd segment	3rd segment	4th segment
Index investing	7.7E-05	4.3E-04	2.4E-04	6.0E-05	1.5E-04	-1.5E-04
Minimum variance optimization	1.2E-04	6.0E-04	2.4E-04	3.0E-04	2.2E-04	-2.7E-04
Sharpe ratio optimization	3.1E-04	1.8E-03	2.5E-04	5.3E-04	4.4E-04	2.3E-05
Bayes-Stein optimization	2.7E-04	1.9E-03	4.5E-05	5.3E-04	4.0E-04	1.0E-04
Ledoit-Wolf optimization	8.6E-05	6.2E-04	2.3E-04	2.1E-04	2.0E-04	-2.9E-04
Rebalanced equally weighted portfolio	1.2E-04	6.2E-04	1.6E-04	2.4E-04	2.1E-04	-1.2E-04
Equal risk contribution portfolio	1.1E-04	5.4E-04	1.4E-04	2.3E-04	2.0E-04	-1.4E-04
Most diversified portfolio	1.7E-04	9.0E-04	1.6E-04	2.9E-04	2.3E-04	2.1E-05
Inverse volatility portfolio	1.0E-04	5.1E-04	1.4E-04	2.2E-04	2.0E-04	-1.6E-04
Diversified risk parity portfolio	9.7E-05	5.1E-04	1.3E-04	2.1E-04	1.9E-04	-1.5E-04

Table 24: Mean return

2 The colour graduation provides the relative performance of the investment strategies within the respective dataset. The brighter the colour the better the strategy. This applies for the entire paper.

Figure 2 below shows the cumulative results of the mean return for the continuous daily dataset.

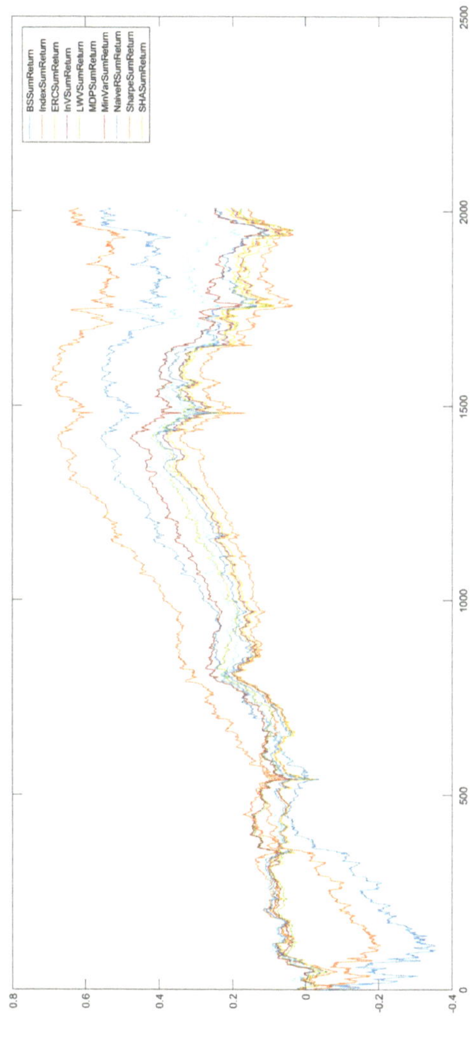

Figure 2: Overview of cumulative returns (complete timeframe daily dataset)

3.2.2.2.2 Variance

In modern portfolio theory, risk is directly associated with the volatility of the return series (Evensky, 1997). The return dispersion or volatility is mathematically expressed via variance, which measures the variability of realized returns around an average level (Radcliffe, 1987). Portfolio variance is calculated as:

$$VAR = \sigma^2 = \sum_{i=1}^{m} \sum_{j=1}^{n} \omega_i \omega_j \sigma_{ij} \tag{56}$$

being the squared standard deviation:

$$\sigma = \sqrt{\frac{\sum_{i=1}^{m} (r_i - R)^2}{m}} \tag{57}$$

Tables 25 and 26 below provide the results for variance and the corresponding bootstrap test.

Variance	daily	weekly	1st segment	2nd segment	3rd segment	4th segment
Index investing	2.70E-05	1.51E-04	3.06E-05	2.12E-05	2.12E-05	3.50E-05
Minimum variance optimization	1.77E-05	1.25E-04	1.41E-05	1.37E-05	1.63E-05	2.64E-05
Sharpe ratio optimization	4.23E-05	2.72E-04	6.86E-05	2.06E-05	1.94E-05	6.05E-05
Bayes-Stein optimization	6.76E-05	3.29E-04	1.55E-04	1.96E-05	1.85E-05	7.71E-05
Ledoit-Wolf optimization	1.79E-05	1.36E-04	1.46E-05	1.45E-05	1.66E-05	2.60E-05
Rebalanced equally weighted portfolio	2.71E-05	1.66E-04	2.28E-05	2.25E-05	2.22E-05	4.09E-05
Equal risk contribution portfolio	2.55E-05	1.54E-04	2.13E-05	2.08E-05	2.08E-05	3.90E-05
Most diversified portfolio	2.71E-05	1.64E-04	2.17E-05	1.82E-05	1.97E-05	4.87E-05
Inverse volatility portfolio	2.57E-05	1.54E-04	2.17E-05	2.12E-05	2.13E-05	3.86E-05
Diversified risk parity portfolio	2.59E-05	1.58E-04	2.15E-05	2.07E-05	2.07E-05	4.05E-05

Table 25: Variance

Daily data variance bootstrap test for statical significance	Index investing	Minimum variance optimization	Sharpe ratio optimization	Bayes-Stein optimization	Ledoit-Wolf optimization	Rebalanced equally weighted portfolio	Equal risk contribution portfolio	Most diversified portfolio	Inverse volatility portfolio	Diversified risk parity portfolio
Index investing	-	0	0	0	0	0	0	0	0	0
Minimum variance optimization	0	-	0	0	0	0	0	0	0	0
Sharpe ratio optimization	0	0	-	0	0	0	0	0	0	0
Bayes-Stein optimization	0	0	0	-	0	0	0	0	0	0
Ledoit-Wolf optimization	0	0	0	0	-	0	0	0	0	0
Rebalanced equally weighted portfolio	0	0	0	0	0	-	0	0	0	0
Equal risk contribution portfolio	0	0	0	0	0	0	-	0	0	0
Most diversified portfolio	0	0	0	0	0	0	0	-	0	0
Inverse volatility portfolio	0	0	0	0	0	0	0	0	-	0
Diversified risk parity portfolio	0	0	0	0	0	0	0	0	0	-

Table 26: Variance bootstrap
(complete timeframe daily dataset)

3.2.2.2.3 Sharpe ratio

The Sharpe ratio measures the excess return of an investment per unit of risk (Poddig, Dichtl, & Petersmeier, 2008). It compares average portfolio excess return to its standard deviation and is one of the most common tools for comparing portfolios (Morey & Vinod, 2001). Sharpe ratio is defined as (Sharpe, 1966):

$$SR = \frac{R - r_f}{\sigma} \tag{58}$$

As the aim of the Sharpe ratio in this paper is to compare different portfolios on the basis of reward to variability, the risk-free rate is excluded, resulting in the modified Sharpe ratio:

$$\text{modified } SR = \frac{R}{\sigma} \tag{59}$$

following Murphy (1999). Tables 27 and 28 below show the results for the Sharpe ratio and the corresponding bootstrap test.

Sharpe ratio	daily	weekly	1st segment	2nd segment	3rd segment	4th segment
Index investing	0.0148	0.0347	0.0442	0.0126	0.0322	negative
Minimum variance optimization	0.0288	0.0541	0.0637	0.0810	0.0549	negative
Sharpe ratio optimization	0.0477	0.1079	0.0305	0.1177	0.1009	0.0030
Bayes-Stein optimization	0.0324	0.1050	0.0036	0.1191	0.0939	0.0116
Ledoit-Wolf optimization	0.0203	0.0530	0.0607	0.0553	0.0482	negative
Rebalanced equally weighted portfolio	0.0236	0.0483	0.0329	0.0515	0.0439	negative
Equal risk contribution portfolio	0.0211	0.0437	0.0308	0.0500	0.0429	negative
Most diversified portfolio	0.0336	0.0703	0.0343	0.0671	0.0521	0.0030
Inverse volatility portfolio	0.0198	0.0411	0.0302	0.0484	0.0428	negative
Diversified risk parity portfolio	0.0198	0.0406	0.0303	0.0490	0.0435	negative

Table 27: Sharpe ratio

Daily data Sharpe ratio bootstrap test for statical significance	Index investing	Minimum variance optimization	Sharpe ratio optimization	Bayes-Stein optimization	Ledoit-Wolf optimization	Rebalanced equally weighted portfolio	Equal risk contribution portfolio	Most diversified portfolio	Inverse volatility portfolio	Diversified risk parity portfolio
Index investing	-	0	0	0	0	0	0	0	0	0
Minimum variance optimization	0	-	0	0	0	0	0	0	0	0
Sharpe ratio optimization	0	0	-	0	0	0	0	0	0	0
Bayes-Stein optimization	0	0	0	-	0	0	0	0	0	0
Ledoit-Wolf optimization	0	0	0	0	-	0	0	0	0	0
Rebalanced equally weighted portfolio	0	0	0	0	0	-	0	0	0	0
Equal risk contribution portfolio	0	0	0	0	0	0	-	0	0	0
Most diversified portfolio	0	0	0	0	0	0	0	-	0	0
Inverse volatility portfolio	0	0	0	0	0	0	0	0	-	0
Diversified risk parity portfolio	0	0	0	0	0	0	0	0	0	-

Table 28: Sharpe ratio bootstrap
(complete timeframe daily dataset)

Figure 3 below shows the risk-return profiles of the investment strategies for the continuous daily dataset.

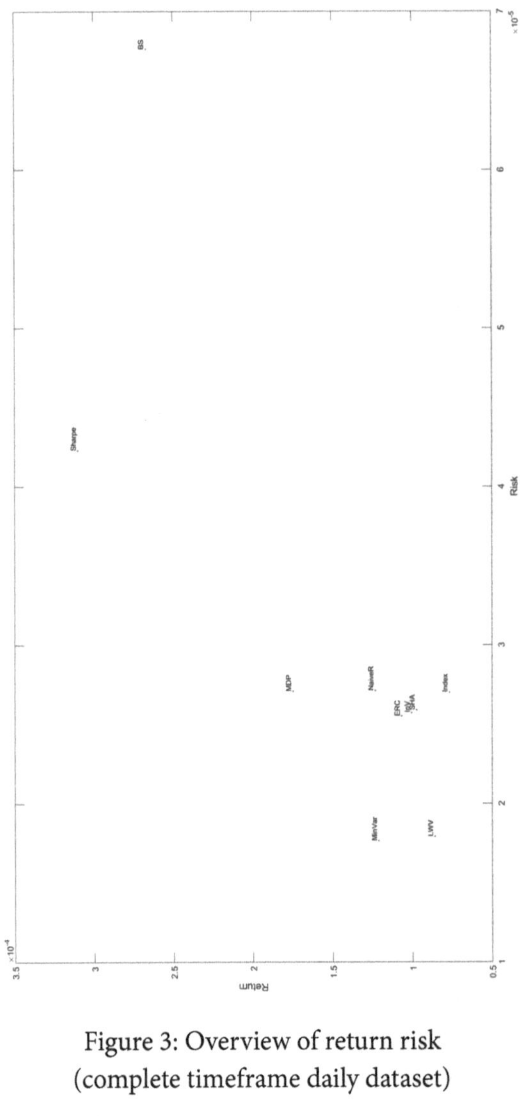

Figure 3: Overview of return risk
(complete timeframe daily dataset)

3.2.2.2.4 Value at risk

Value at risk is defined as the maximum potential negative change (downside risk) in the value of a portfolio of financial instruments with a given probability over a certain horizon, or from a different perspective, the one-sided confidence interval on potential portfolio losses over a specific period of time, answering the question of what is the highest amount that can be lost on a particular investment (J.P. Morgan, 1994; Hallerbach, 2002). Value at risk at $1 - \alpha$ is mathematically defined as:

$$\Pr\left(\Delta V \leq -VaR_{1-\alpha}\right) = \alpha \tag{60}$$

or in other terms as:

$$VaR_{1-\alpha} = -F^{-1}(\alpha) \tag{61}$$

with three confidence levels: 90%, 95%, and 99%. Table 29 below provides the results for value at risk for the continuous daily dataset.

Value at risk (5%)	daily	weekly	1st segment	2nd segment	3rd segment	4th segment
Index investing	0.0085	0.0198	0.0089	0.0075	0.0074	0.0099
Minimum variance optimization	0.0068	0.0178	0.0059	0.0058	0.0064	0.0087
Sharpe ratio optimization	0.0104	0.0253	0.0134	0.0069	0.0068	0.0128
Bayes-Stein optimization	0.0133	0.0279	0.0204	0.0068	0.0067	0.0143
Ledoit-Wolf optimization	0.0069	0.0186	0.0060	0.0060	0.0065	0.0087
Rebalanced equally weighted portfolio	0.0084	0.0206	0.0077	0.0076	0.0075	0.0106
Equal risk contribution portfolio	0.0082	0.0198	0.0075	0.0073	0.0073	0.0104
Most diversified portfolio	0.0084	0.0202	0.0075	0.0067	0.0071	0.0115
Inverse volatility portfolio	0.0082	0.0199	0.0075	0.0074	0.0074	0.0104
Diversified risk parity portfolio	0.0083	0.0202	0.0075	0.0073	0.0073	0.0106

Table 29: Value at risk

3.2.2.2.5 Certainty equivalent return

The certainty equivalent return is defined as the risk-free rate of return that a risk-averse investor is willing to accept rather than adopting a risky portfolio strategy (DeMiguel, Garlappi, & Uppal, 2009). The certainty equivalent return is defined as:

$$CER = R - \frac{\gamma}{2}\sigma^2 \tag{62}$$

The risk-aversion coefficient γ is defined here as a rolling window from 1 to 10 in steps of 1. However, comparison of the investment strategies is conducted using $\gamma = 1$, following DeMiguel, Garlappi and Uppal (2009). Table 30 below shows the results for the certainty equivalent return.

Certainty equivalent return ($\gamma = 1$)	daily	weekly	1st segment	2nd segment	3rd segment	4th segment
Index investing	6.3E-05	3.5E-04	2.3E-04	5.0E-05	1.4E-04	-1.7E-04
Minimum variance optimization	1.1E-04	5.4E-04	2.3E-04	2.9E-04	2.1E-04	-2.8E-04
Sharpe ratio optimization	2.9E-04	1.6E-03	2.2E-04	5.2E-04	4.3E-04	-1.0E-05
Bayes-Stein optimization	2.3E-04	1.7E-03	-3.0E-05	5.2E-04	3.9E-04	6.0E-05
Ledoit-Wolf optimization	7.7E-05	5.5E-04	2.2E-04	2.0E-04	1.9E-04	-3.0E-04
Rebalanced equally weighted portfolio	1.1E-04	5.4E-04	1.5E-04	2.3E-04	2.0E-04	-1.4E-04
Equal risk contribution portfolio	9.4E-05	4.7E-04	1.3E-04	2.2E-04	1.9E-04	-1.6E-04
Most diversified portfolio	1.6E-04	8.2E-04	1.5E-04	2.8E-04	2.2E-04	-3.1E-04
Inverse volatility portfolio	8.8E-05	4.3E-04	1.3E-04	2.1E-04	1.9E-04	-1.8E-04
Diversified risk parity portfolio	8.4E-05	4.4E-04	1.2E-04	2.0E-04	1.8E-04	-1.7E-04

Table 30: Certainty equivalent return

Figure 4 below provides the results for the certainty equivalent return for the continuous daily dataset.

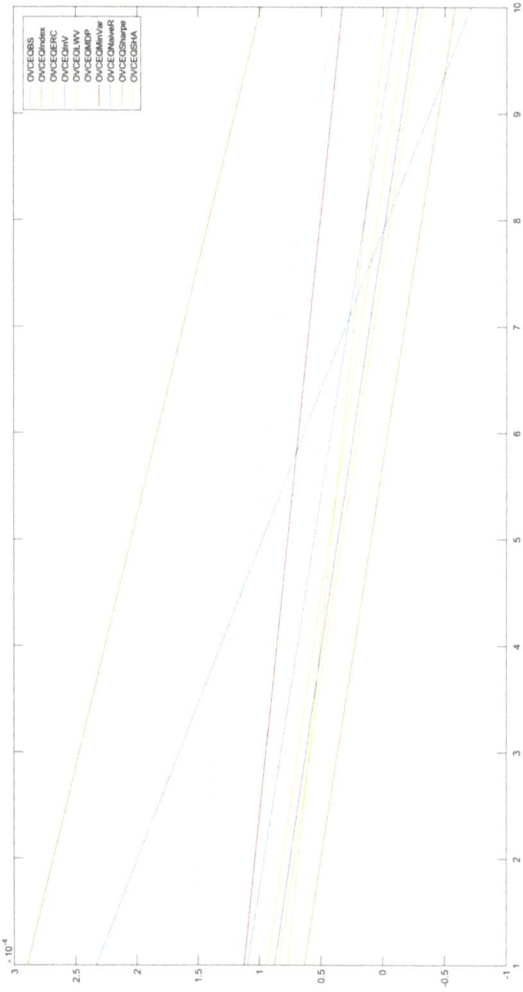

Figure 4: Overview of certainty equivalent return (complete timeframe daily dataset)

3.2.2.2.6 Diversification ratio

The diversification ratio embodies the very nature of diversification and is defined as the ratio of a portfolio's weighted average volatility to its overall volatility (Choueifaty, Froidure, & Reynier, 2013). The concept corresponds to the following expression:

$$DR = \frac{1}{m}\sum_{i=1}^{m}\frac{\sum_{j=1}^{n}\omega_j\sigma_j}{\sigma} = \frac{1}{m}\sum_{i=1}^{m}\frac{\omega^T\sigma}{\sqrt{\omega^T\Sigma\omega}} \tag{63}$$

for the average diversification ratio. Exploiting the risk-reduction effect of correlation, the ratio measures precisely the degree of diversification in the portfolio resulting from combination of individual assets (Choueifaty & Coignard, 2008). Table 31 below presents the results of the diversification ratio.

Diversification ratio	daily	weekly	1st segment	2nd segment	3rd segment	4th segment
Index investing	1.0000	1.0000	1.0000	1.0000	1.0000	1.0000
Minimum variance optimization	1.1165	1.0932	1.0284	1.0952	1.1892	1.0151
Sharpe ratio optimization	0.9306	0.9479	0.6258	0.9296	0.9919	0.9467
Bayes-Stein optimization	0.9145	0.9524	0.5377	0.9575	1.0323	0.8823
Ledoit-Wolf optimization	1.0614	0.9678	0.9919	1.0106	1.1239	0.9874
Rebalanced equally weighted portfolio	1.2883	1.2902	1.1920	1.2486	1.3121	1.2658
Equal risk contribution portfolio	1.3000	1.3049	1.2030	1.2625	1.3238	1.2661
Most diversified portfolio	1.4016	1.4296	1.2762	1.3526	1.4448	1.3755
Inverse volatility portfolio	1.2778	1.2763	1.1939	1.2496	1.2837	1.2469
Diversified risk parity portfolio	1.2968	1.3010	1.1926	1.2577	1.3241	1.2549

Table 31: Diversification ratio

Figure 5 below provides the results for the diversification ratio for the continuous daily dataset.

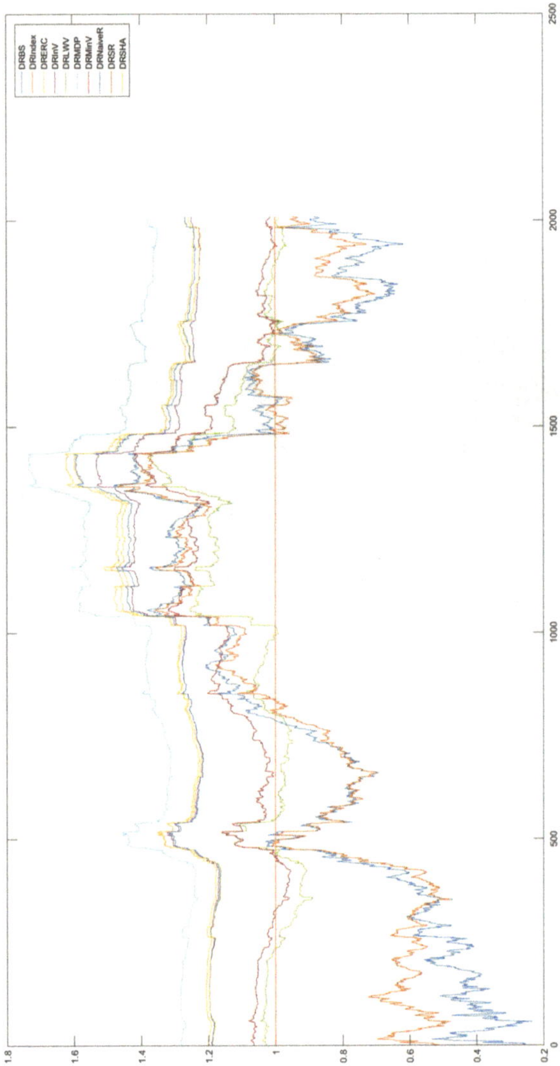

Figure 5: Overview of diversification ratio (complete timeframe daily dataset)

3.2.2.2.7 Turnover

Turnover is defined as the measure of how much holdings in a portfolio change over a specific time period relative to portfolio size (Taylor, 2006). It is mathematically expressed as the average sum of the absolute value of trades across all available assets over the entire invested period (DeMiguel, Garlappi, & Uppal, 2009):

$$\text{Turnover} = \sum_{i=1}^{m} \sum_{j=1}^{n} \left(\left| \omega_{j,i} - \omega_{j,i-1+} \right| \right) \tag{64}$$

High turnover is directly related to additional costs, which leaves a promising strategy potentially unprofitable (Kremer, Talmaciu, & Paterlini, 2018). Table 32 below shows the results for turnover.

Turnover	daily	weekly	1st segment	2nd segment	3rd segment	4th segment
Index investing	1.0	1.0	1.0	1.0	1.0	1.0
Minimum variance optimization	72.2	80.5	20.3	19.3	19.6	19.6
Sharpe ratio optimization	375.7	189.7	159.4	73.6	46.3	106.8
Bayes-Stein optimization	506.8	229.9	267.5	71.6	40.7	136.7
Ledoit-Wolf optimization	59.0	50.5	16.7	14.5	16.9	16.9
Rebalanced equally weighted portfolio	11.6	6.4	3.6	3.5	3.3	4.3
Equal risk contribution portfolio	8.5	5.9	2.8	2.6	2.8	3.2
Most diversified portfolio	27.7	22.9	7.2	7.3	9.0	7.1
Inverse volatility portfolio	8.3	5.5	2.8	2.6	2.7	3.2
Diversified risk parity portfolio	11.4	11.2	3.7	3.1	3.5	4.0

Table 32: Turnover

3.3 Results

Table 33 below provides an overview of the aggregated results of the asset allocation strategies, with the continuous daily dataset serving as input data. Potential outperformance is quantified according to a set of measurements that consider mainly return, risk, and their combination from different perspectives. As further explanation, results showing the effect of the quantitative asset allocation strategies in the context of the set of measurement techniques applied to validate and collate potential outperforming portfolios, as well as the bootstrap validation of the variance and Sharpe ratio, were given below the measurement subsections.

Daily data	Mean return	Variance	Sharpe ratio	Value at risk	Certainty equivalent return	Diversification ratio	Turnover
Index investing	7.7E-05	2.70E-05	0.0148	0.0085	6.3E-05	1.0000	1.0
Minimum variance optimization	1.2E-04	1.77E-05	0.0288	0.0068	1.1E-04	1.1165	72.2
Sharpe ratio optimization	3.1E-04	4.23E-05	0.0477	0.0104	2.9E-04	0.9306	375.7
Bayes-Stein optimization	2.7E-04	6.76E-05	0.0324	0.0133	2.3E-04	0.9145	506.8
Ledoit-Wolf optimization	8.6E-05	1.79E-05	0.0203	0.0069	7.7E-05	1.0614	59.0
Rebalanced equally weighted portfolio	1.2E-04	2.71E-05	0.0236	0.0084	1.1E-04	1.2883	11.6
Equal risk contribution portfolio	1.1E-04	2.55E-05	0.0211	0.0082	9.4E-05	1.3000	8.5
Most diversified portfolio	1.7E-04	2.71E-05	0.0336	0.0084	1.6E-04	1.4016	27.7
Inverse volatility portfolio	1.0E-04	2.57E-05	0.0198	0.0082	8.8E-05	1.2778	8.3
Diversified risk parity portfolio	9.7E-05	2.59E-05	0.0198	0.0083	8.4E-05	1.2968	11.4

Table 33: Results overview for daily data

The main research hypothesis H_0 (1) is clearly not rejected, as the overall assessment provides the consistent outcome that the questioned transformation is possible. Both the selected quantitative techniques of portfolio optimization and its extensions, as well as the risk-minimizing, long-only approaches, entirely outperform the benchmark of index investing (the weak-form market-inefficient TASI) in terms of mean return, Sharpe ratio, and certainty equivalent return. The index is ranked last. In addition, there is mostly significant distance in the actual values of these measurements. Further, in the solely risk-related measurements of variance, value at risk, and diversification ratio, the index investing benchmark is ranked at the lower end of the scale, supporting acceptance of H_0 (1). This is in consideration of the fact that the TASI, as the superordinate index, benefits from an averaging effect and gains from the diversification effect of negatively correlated constituents significantly more than the subindices (Lintner, 1965). Only regarding the measurement turnover rate is the index ranked first with regard to the initial purchase; consequently it is more cost-efficient (Poddig, Brinkmann, & Seiler, 2005); but this is not the focus of this paper. We may conclude that within the timeframe of 2007 to 2017, for continuous daily input data, the possibility exists that proven weak-form market inefficiencies of the TASI can be exploited on a systematic and continuous basis by treating the subindices of the TASI as asset classes upon which mechanical trading rules are applied to generate outperforming portfolios.

To address hypothesis H_0 (2) regarding a direct linkage between weak-form market inefficiencies and the possibility of generating outperforming portfolios via quantitative active investment strategies, the results of the four segments of the daily dataset are examined on an individual basis via average deviation of the benchmark index from the active asset allocation strategies. In the first segment, which covers the timeframe of the financial crisis, where the TASI is found to be weak-form market efficient or at least shows the relative peak of its weak-form market efficiency (Abdmoulah, 2010; Arshad, Rizvi, Ghani,

& Duasa, 2016), the TASI outperforms the average quantitative investment strategy significantly in measurements of mean return, variance, Sharpe ratio, value at risk, and certainty equivalent return. Regarding the diversification ratio, where the TASI is consistently outperformed in all four segments, and turnover, where the TASI consistently outperforms the active asset allocation strategies, the relative best results are achieved by the benchmark. The outcome for the second segment, where some degree of weak-form market efficiency prevails, is that the TASI is substantially outperformed by the quantitative active investment strategies in terms of mean return, variance, Sharpe ratio, value at risk, certainty equivalent return, and diversification ratio. The average deviation of turnover where the TASI dominates is less than half the value of the first segment. From an overall perspective, the active investment strategies performed relatively better compared to the benchmark of the second segment. Regarding the third segment, in which the TASI is found to be weak-form market-inefficient, the index investment strategy was, apart from the previously mentioned turnover ratio, beaten by the asset allocation strategies in every measurement. However, the relative outperformance in the interspaces of the values was, with the exception of the diversification ratio, relatively lower compared to the second segment, in which the degree of weak-form market efficiency was higher. In the fourth segment, where, similar to the second segment, some degree of weak-form market efficiency was discovered, the average quantitative investment strategy outperformed the TASI in mean return, certainty equivalent return, and diversification, with the relative highest level for mean return over all four segments and the relative lowest levels for certainty equivalent return and diversification ratio over the last three segments. For variance and value at risk and exclusively evaluating risk, the active asset allocation strategies showed weaker performance compared to the TASI, especially regarding value at risk, where the relative average deviation was the highest of all four segments. An assessment of the Sharpe ratio is, due partly to negative values, not feasible in this segment. Table 34 below presents average deviation of index investing from the asset allocation strategies for the entire set of measurements for the segmented daily dataset, together with the degree of weak-form market efficiency.

Daily segmented data	Average devidaton of index investing from asset allocation strategies			
	1st segment	2nd segment	3rd segment	4th segment
Mean return	-7.76E-05	2.49E-04	1.07E-04	3.90E-05
Variance	9.57E-06	-2.14E-06	-1.70E-06	9.20E-06
Sharpe ratio	-0.0090	0.0584	0.0259	N/A
Value at risk	4.21E-04	-6.64E-04	-4.25E-04	10.14E-04
Certainty equivalent return	-8.24E-05	2.50E-04	1.07E-04	3.44E-05
Diversification ratio	0.0268	0.1515	0.3813	0.1465
Turnover	52.8	21.0	15.1	32.5

Degree of efficiency*	+	0	-	0

* As given in the paper "How informational efficient is the Saudi Stock Exchange?".

Table 34: Results overview for segmentation

By examining results for the four segments jointly, we conclude that the alignment of ability to predict future prices from past price changes leading to outperforming active investment strategies with the graduating degree of market efficiency of the TASI in the segmented datasets is given only within limits. The proposition of H_0 (2) is true for the first segment and holds for the second segment; however, in the third segment, the relative outperformance of the active investment strategies contradicts the hypothesis, and in the fourth segment, the outcome of variance and value at risk counters acceptance of the hypothesis. At the same time, we show that in a weak-form market efficiency environment, the TASI beats active investment strategies, and vice versa for a weak-form market-inefficient environment. However, H_0 (2) does not hold for segments with some degree of weak-form market efficiency, as outperformance of the active asset allocation strategies in the second segment with some degree of weak-form market efficiency surmounts the outperformance in the third segment with weak-form market inefficiency. Further, the solely risk-related variance and value at risk in the fourth segment favors the passive index investing strategy, not allowing for the conclusion that the TASI in segments with some degree of weak-form market efficiency is consistently outperformed by quantitative asset allocation strategies regarding all measurements. This means that only in a weak-form market efficiency environment does the TASI outperform the active investment strategies.

Table 35 below presents an overview of the aggregated results of the asset allocation strategies with the weekly dataset as input data, where potential outperformance is enumerated according to a set of measurements that consider mainly return, risk and their combination from multiple viewpoints.

Weekly data	Mean return	Variance	Sharpe ratio	Value at risk	Certainty equivalent return	Diversification ratio	Turnover
Index investing	4.3E-04	1.51E-04	0.0347	0.0198	3.5E-04	1.0000	1.0
Minimum variance optimization	6.0E-04	1.25E-04	0.0541	0.0178	5.4E-04	1.0932	80.5
Sharpe ratio optimization	1.8E-03	2.72E-04	0.1079	0.0253	1.6E-03	0.9479	189.7
Bayes-Stein optimization	1.9E-03	3.29E-04	0.1050	0.0279	1.7E-03	0.9524	229.9
Ledoit-Wolf optimization	6.2E-04	1.36E-04	0.0530	0.0186	5.5E-04	0.9678	50.5
Rebalanced equally weighted portfolio	6.2E-04	1.66E-04	0.0483	0.0206	5.4E-04	1.2902	6.4
Equal risk contribution portfolio	5.4E-04	1.54E-04	0.0437	0.0198	4.7E-04	1.3049	5.9
Most diversified portfolio	9.0E-04	1.64E-04	0.0703	0.0202	8.2E-04	1.4296	22.9
Inverse volatility portfolio	5.1E-04	1.54E-04	0.0411	0.0199	4.3E-04	1.2763	5.5
Diversified risk parity portfolio	5.1E-04	1.58E-04	0.0406	0.0202	4.4E-04	1.3010	11.2

Table 35: Results overview for weekly data

Hypothesis H_0 (3), which assesses the existence of a possible relation between the degree of possible transformation and the degree of discovered market efficiency in a data frequency-dependent perspective by utilizing weak-form market-inefficient daily and weak-form efficient weekly input data from the same time horizon in comparison, must be rejected, as the outperformance results of active asset allocation strategies compared to the TASI are analogous in ranks and relative value interspaces for both data frequencies regarding mean return, Sharpe ratio, certainty equivalent return, and diversification ratio. As previously discussed, the same applies to measurement turnover. Partial acceptance is given only by valuation of risk-related variance and value at risk, where the TASI is ranked, in both cases, third in a weak-form market-efficient environment compared to sixth and seventh rankings in a weak-form market-inefficient environment. Consequently, the data allow for the proposition that the influence of weak-form market efficiency is more dominant for the risk aspect by comparing the performance of active and passive investment strategies.

3.4 Conclusion

This paper documents empirical evidence for propositions in several academic papers on the implications of weak-form market inefficiencies found in the Tadawul. In weak-form inefficient markets, the ability of active investment strategies to outperform the benchmark must be provable and measurable (Jamaani & Roca, 2015; Asiri & Alzeera, 2013; Bley, 2011). At the same time, the absence of weak-form market efficiency must be confirmed by inverting the order of reasoning (Malkiel, 2003). This work provides investors with insights on the possibility of generating abnormal risk-adjusted returns within the investment horizon of the recently emerging market revalued Tadawul on a systematic and continuous basis by applying mechanical trading rules. Further, the results from selected quantitative techniques of portfolio optimization from modern portfolio theory and its extensions, together with risk-minimizing long-only approaches by treating the subindices of the TASI as asset classes and benchmarking their optimal attributed weightings against the TASI in consideration of different measurement perspectives, provide initial indications of potentially promising investment opportunities. In addition, insights on the interplay between the degree of efficiency and the magnitude of the potential outperformance allow for business cycle-dependent tailored investment opportunities. Policy makers should use these results to further enhance efforts toward market efficiency by overcoming information asymmetry. Vehicles and instruments aiding this development include, among others, market liberalization, privatization, diversification of financial services, improvement of the investment climate with widespread institutional trading, and structural reforms accepting foreign stock ownership (Bley, 2011; Abdmoulah, 2010). Additionally, engagement of sophisticated foreign and domesticated investors seeking risk-adjusted alpha returns through exploitation of market inefficiency will contribute to the weak-form market efficiency of the Tadawul, consequently attracting passive investors (Poddig, Brinkmann, & Seiler, 2005).

This paper is not without limitations. Although we document that the posited transformation of market inefficiencies into abnormal returns through application of quantitative techniques of portfolio optimization works with this dataset with its single investment horizon over one timeframe, this does not imply general validity.

We suggest further research based on a greater variety of investment horizons, such as indices from developed as well as emerging and frontier markets, or testing application over different market cycles with potentially varying degrees of weak-form market efficiency.

4. How dependent are Saudi Arabia's economic sectors on oil price?

We extend the literature on the dependency of the Tadawul on oil price developments by examining individual economic sectors, which, to our best knowledge, has never been a focus, particularly with respect to possible temporal development. Economic sectors are defined as subindices of the TASI, and we utilize the complete timeframe in which the Tadawul contains 15 subindices, that is, 2007 to 2017, together with five consecutive subsets of equal length considering both long- and short-term relations. We address the fact that various economic sectors may be affected differently by oil price changes and the possible changes in these dependencies over time. We find a significant and strong relation between crude oil prices and the TASI. Further, we provide empirical evidence from several economic sectors that are long- and short-term highly independent of oil price developments. The majority of economic sectors, especially the petro sector, are highly linked to oil price developments. Over time, the relation of the Tadawul to crude oil prices intensifies in the short- and long-term perspective, despite efforts of the Government of Saudi Arabia to diversify the nation's economy away from oil.

4.1 Literature review

Fouquau (2009) finds no short-term relation between oil price changes and the Tadawul after examining both linear and nonlinear relations for weekly data from 2005 to 2008. Together with Arouri, this author then used monthly data from 1996 to 2007 to show evidence of an asymmetric, long-term relation between oil prices and the Tadawul using classic and asymmetric cointegration to focus on both linear and nonlinear dependencies (Arouri & Fouquau, 2011). Using monthly data from 1996 to 2007, Arouri and Rault (2012) applied a bootstrap panel cointegration technique together with a seemingly unrelated regression method and discovered a strong, long-term relation between OPEC oil prices and the Tadawul. Arouri et al. (2012) published evidence of short-term positive links between oil prices and the Tadawul, while the cointegration results showed that there is no long-term link between oil prices and the Tadawul. Akoum et al. (2012) utilized the wavelet coherency methodology to discover long-term dependencies between oil prices and the Tadawul, while no short-term dependencies could be validated between 2002 and 2011 for weekly data.

The first empirical research on return interaction between oil prices and five selected economic sectors of the Tadawul was conducted by Jouini with weekly data for the period 2007 to 2011. For short-term dependencies, the unconditional correlation shows a strong relation between oil prices and TASI, and on the sectoral level, a strong relation between oil prices and industrial investment and banks. However, telecom, insurance, and energy are less affected by short-term oil price changes. In the long term, no significant linkage between oil price and stock market sectors in Saudi Arabia could be observed via the VAR-GARCH process (Jouini, 2013).

Another empirical research paper covering the relation of oil prices and four selected economic sectors of the Tadawul considered daily data from 2009 to 2012, providing significant evidence of a short-term relation. All conditional correlations between oil price, the stock market index, and the sector indexes of banking, telecom, industrial, and cement suggest strong positive interdependence (Almohaimeed & Harrathi, 2013).

Samontaray et al. (2014) show a positive and significant correlation between the West Texas Intermediate (WTI) price and the TASI using monthly data from 2003 to 2013. Alqattan and Alhayky (2016) find a significant short-term relation and no evidence of a long-term relation between oil prices and the stock market index of Saudi Arabia in the period 2006 to 2015 with monthly frequency using the ARDL method. Dependent on positive or negative oil price changes, Marashdeh and Afandi (2017) find ambiguous results regarding the effect on the Tadawul employing the VECM model for monthly data from 2000 to 2015.

Mensi (2019) investigates the dependency between oil prices and all 15 economic sectors of the Tadawul for the period 2007 to 2017 with daily frequency. In the short term, the petrochemical sector showed the highest correlation with crude oil. In contrast, the lowest correlation was with media and publishing industries. The aggregated index ranked second, which indicates the strong influence of the petrochemical sector on the stock index of Saudi Arabia. Using the wavelets coherency methodology as the core research concept, co-movement between oil prices and the TASI was considered weak over the long term. On sectoral level, the long-term relation peaked for the petrochemical sector, while hotel and tourism are low-dependent with the oil market.

The VAR methodology framework analysis executed by Rahman (2020) shows a long-run relation between crude oil prices and stock prices on the Tadawul, while no short-run co-movement is found between them for daily data in the period 2000 to 2017.

Further research on the short- and long-term relation between oil prices and the Tadawul is justified by the deviating and inconclusive results of the studies summarized here. Evidence from sectoral interaction is sparse, while data segmentation adds the dimension of research targeting possible temporal developments, contributing to the literature.

4.2 Data and methodology

We test for short- and long-term relation of crude oil prices with the Tadawul through the hypothesis of a positively correlated, short-term relation and significant long-term dependencies. For oil prices, we follow the majority of previous research and use the WTI (Rahman, 2020; Mensi, 2019; Samontaray, Nugali, & Sasidhar, 2014); the Tadawul is represented by the TASI and its 15 subindices, which represent economic sectors. Our methods include the Pearson's linear correlation coefficient for short-term co-movement and the Johansen cointegration test for long-term co-movement. Using the same approaches, we split the dataset into five consecutive subsets of equal length to investigate time-dependent change.

4.2.1 Data

The input data for the empirical analysis contain the WTI, the TASI and its 15 subindex datasets at daily frequency from 06.01.2007 to 05.01.2017 (that is, until reclassification in accordance with the Global Industry Classification Standard), resulting in 2610 daily time-dependent data points (Saudi Stock Exchange, 2017). Further, the dataset at daily frequency is split into five segments containing approximately 522 time-dependent data points. The sectoral overview of the 15 subindices is provided in Table 36 below (Saudi Stock Exchange, 2016).

Tadawul and subindices		
Code	Name	Nomenclature paper
SASEIDX	Tadawul	TASI
SASEBNK	Tadawul All Share Banking Index	Subindex 1
SASEPETR	Tadawul All Share Petro Index	Subindex 2
SASECEM	Tadawul All Share Cement Index	Subindex 3
SASERETL	Tadawul All Share Retail Industries Index	Subindex 4
SASEINS	Tadawul All Share Insurance Index	Subindex 5
SASETEL	Tadawul All Share Telecommunications Index	Subindex 6
SASEREAL	Tadawul All Share Real Estate Development Industries Index	Subindex 7
SASEBULD	Tadawul All Share Building & Construction Index	Subindex 8
SASEMINV	Tadawul All Share Multi-Investment Index	Subindex 9
SASEINDI	Tadawul All Share Industrial Investment Industries Index	Subindex 10
SASEAGRI	Tadawul All Share Agriculture & Food Industries Index	Subindex 11
SASEENER	Tadawul All Share Energy & Utilities Industries Index	Subindex 12
SASEMEDI	Tadawul All Share Media & Publishing Industries Index	Subindex 13
SASETRAN	Tadawul All Share Transport Industries Index	Subindex 14
SASEHOTE	Tadawul All Share Hotel & Tourism Industries Index	Subindex 15

Table 36: Subindex sectoral overview

Table 37 below reports descriptive statistics for the TASI together with its 15 subindices.

Descriptive statistics (daily 06.01.2007-05.01.2017)

	DS					
	mean return	sigma	skewness	kurtosis	Jarque-Bera test	p-value (5%)
WTI	-0.0001828	0.0104	0.0444	6.96370	1709	0.000
TASI	-0.0001689	0.0061	-1.2890	16.5789	20775	0.000
Subindex 1	-0.0000639	0.0063	-0.5965	15.4124	16910	0.000
Subindex 2	0.0000085	0.0081	-0.9475	14.0572	13686	0.000
Subindex 3	-0.0000452	0.0057	-1.1914	20.7560	34903	0.000
Subindex 4	0.0001137	0.0065	-1.0142	16.7014	20863	0.000
Subindex 5	-0.0000080	0.0089	-0.7710	9.64500	5061	0.000
Subindex 6	-0.0001131	0.0066	-1.1384	17.4280	23202	0.000
Subindex 7	0.0000525	0.0075	-0.5064	11.5852	8127	0.000
Subindex 8	-0.0001524	0.0081	-1.5267	16.4384	20653	0.000
Subindex 9	-0.0001042	0.0086	-0.8756	12.1452	9429	0.000
Subindex 10	0.0000370	0.0079	-1.1894	11.7582	8957	0.000
Subindex 11	0.0000840	0.0069	-1.1945	15.0322	16365	0.000
Subindex 12	0.0000778	0.0066	0.1605	13.6889	12436	0.000
Subindex 13	-0.0001114	0.0101	-0.1933	10.5038	6140	0.000
Subindex 14	0.0000710	0.0085	-0.8060	12.5376	10175	0.000
Subindex 15	0.0000980	0.0099	-0.1924	13.8522	12824	0.000

Table 37: Descriptive statistics

We use log first differences for the short-term correlation analysis and log data for the long-term cointegration analysis. The observed data are mostly negatively skewed with long left tails and high kurtosis, indicating fat tails and high peaks. Accordingly, the normality of the distribution is rejected by the Jarque-Bera test for all indices (Jarque & Bera, 1987) and high systemic risk is presumed (Cont, Moussa, & Santos, 2013).

4.2.2 Methodology

The following subsections set forth the methodological background for testing short- and long-term relations.

4.2.2.1 Correlation

Correlation measures the short-term relation between two time series; this is among the most common and useful statistical techniques (Ahlgren, Jarneving, & Rousseau, 2003). The most familiar method is the Pearson correlation, widely used as a measure of the strength of linear dependence between two variables and mathematically given as (Pearson, 1920):

$$\hat{p} = \frac{\sum_i (x_i - \bar{x})\left(y_i - \bar{y}\right)}{\sqrt{\sum_i (x_i - \bar{x})^2}\sqrt{\sum_i \left(y_i - \bar{y}\right)^2}} \tag{65}$$

Via correlation, it can be assessed whether the relation is direct or inverse as well as its strength. However, correlation does not imply causality and does not provide an indication about linearity (Anscombe, 1973; Granger, 1969).

4.2.2.2 Cointegration

The cointegration method allows us to analyze non-stationary and trend-behaving time series with regard to long-term equilibrium (Shapiro, 1986). Using cointegration vectors to study the long-term relation between time series originated from Engle and Granger (1987). Johansen (1988) further refined statistical analysis of cointegrating vectors by introducing a new method adding maximum likelihood estimation to the Engle-Granger method, which became the most common and precise cointegration test, known as the Johansen test. The increase in precision is due mainly to Johansen's use of maximum likelihood estimation instead of regression analysis, as in the Engle-Granger approach to estimate cointegration relations (Johansen & Juselius, 1990). Johansen's method has another advantage in that it can be used to estimate multiple cointegration relations, while the classical Engle-Granger approach can estimate only one cointegration relation in bi-variate and multivariate cases (Johansen, 2005; Engle, Granger,

& Hallman, 1989). To be cointegrated, the time series data must fulfill certain requirements. The data series must be non-stationary in their levels and stationary in their log differences. Further, they need to be integrated of order 1 and a linear combination of both series must possess a lower integration level while stationary. Fulfillment of these preconditions is validated in Tables 38 and 39 below.

Augmented Dickey-Fuller test (daily 06.01.2007-05.01.2017)

	ADF test level		
	No constant and no trend	Constant and no trend	Constant and trend
WTI	-0.9503	-0.5814	-1.9904
TASI	-0.1818	-1.8771	-1.9201
Subindex 1	-0.5618	-2.3653	-2.3456
Subindex 2	-0.0022	-1.9538	-2.0032
Subindex 3	-0.4396	-1.1857	-1.1603
Subindex 4	0.8446	-0.7621	-1.4996
Subindex 5	-0.1204	-1.908	-1.9226
Subindex 6	-0.9323	-2.043	-2.0206
Subindex 7	0.3182	-0.933	-1.5893
Subindex 8	-1.0036	-1.0874	-1.9609
Subindex 9	-0.695	-1.7916	-1.7396
Subindex 10	0.1876	-2.0722	-2.5989
Subindex 11	0.5756	-1.1612	-2.0434
Subindex 12	0.5801	-1.2487	-3.0193
Subindex 13	-0.6693	-2.5447	-2.4370
Subindex 14	0.3840	-0.9486	-2.1219
Subindex 15	0.4350	-1.1967	-1.2651

* Indicates the rejection of the null hypothesis of a unit root and non stationarity at a 1% level of significance for values below the critical value of -2.58 (no constant and no trend), -3.43 (constant and no trend) and, -3.96 (constant and trend).

Table 38: Stationarity test level data

Augmented Dickey-Fuller test (daily 06.01.2007-05.01.2017)			
	ADF test first difference		
	No constant and no trend	Constant and no trend	Constant and trend
WTI	-49.1674*	-49.1619*	-49.1700*
TASI	-47.1111*	-47.1022*	-47.0935*
Subindex 1	-45.7310*	-45.7257*	-45.7187*
Subindex 2	-48.2808*	-48.2717*	-48.2669*
Subindex 3	-48.2581*	-48.2517*	-48.2435*
Subindex 4	-47.9343*	-47.9400*	-47.9308*
Subindex 5	-46.9852*	-46.9762*	-46.9722*
Subindex 6	-48.1381*	-48.1416*	-48.1348*
Subindex 7	-46.9715*	-46.9652*	-46.9816*
Subindex 8	-47.1022*	-47.1072*	-47.1001*
Subindex 9	-48.8421*	-48.8390*	-48.8338*
Subindex 10	-47.8074*	-47.7996*	-47.7905*
Subindex 11	-47.1257*	-47.1235*	-47.1146*
Subindex 12	-54.1766*	-54.1757*	-54.1933*
Subindex 13	-44.4184*	-44.4140*	-44.4251*
Subindex 14	-49.1674*	-49.1619*	-49.1700*
Subindex 15	-46.8700*	-46.8651*	-46.8590*

* Indicates the rejection of the null hypothesis of a unit root and non stationarity at a 1% level of significance for values below the critical value of -2.58 (no constant and no trend), -3.43 (constant and no trend) and, -3.96 (constant and trend).

Table 39: Stationarity test log differences

The starting point of Johansen's methodology, which we use for our analysis, is the vector autoregression of order p, given as:

$$y_t = \mu + A_1 y_{t-1} + \cdots + A_p y_{t-p} + \epsilon_t, \epsilon_t N\left(+, \sigma^2\right), iid, (t = 1, \dots, T) \tag{66}$$

where y_t is an $n \times 1$ vector of variables that are integrated of order 1, and ϵ_t is an $n \times 1$ vector of innovations. After taking the first differences, the model can be rewritten as:

$$\Delta y_t = \mu + \Pi y_{t-1} + \sum_{i=1}^{p-1} \Gamma_i \Delta y_{t-1} + \epsilon_t \tag{67}$$

with:

$$\Gamma_i = -\sum_{j=i+1}^{p} \mathrm{A}_j, i = 1, \dots, p-1 \tag{68}$$

and:

$$\Pi = \sum_{i=1}^{p} A_j - I \tag{69}$$

where I is the identity matrix (Johansen, 1988). In case the coefficient matrix II has a reduced rank $r < n$, then there exist nxr matrices α and β, each with rank r such that $\Pi = \alpha\beta'$ and $\beta' y_t$ is stationary. The number of cointegrating relations is r, the elements of α are known as the adjustment parameters in the vectors error correlation model with information about the adjustment properties to the long-term equilibrium, and each column of β is a cointegration vector containing information about the long-run cointegration relation. At a given r, the maximum likelihood estimator of β defines the combination of Δy_t with y_{t-1} (Hjalmarsson & Österholm, 2010; Johansen, 1995). Johansen proposes two different likelihood ratio tests based on the null hypothesis of r cointegrating vectors being the trace test with the alternative hypothesis of n cointegrating vectors given by:

$$J_{\text{trace}} = -T \sum_{i=r+1}^{n} \ln\left(1 - \hat{\lambda}_i\right) \tag{70}$$

and the maximum eigenvalue test with the alternative hypothesis or $r + 1$ cointegrating vectors expressed as:

$$J_{\max} = -\mathrm{T}\ln\left(1 - \hat{\lambda}_{r+1}\right) \tag{71}$$

where T is the sample size and $\hat{\lambda}_i$ is the i th-largest canonical correlation. Both tests share the principle that in case the variables are not cointegrated, the rank of matrix Π should be insignificantly different from zero and consequently, the eigenvalues should also be very close to zero (Johansen & Juselius, 1990). Interpretation of the test statistic results is done with respect to the critical values provided by Johansen and Juselius, since the distribution of the maximum likelihood function is not χ^2 but a function of a Standard Brownian Motion (Johansen & Juselius, 2008).

4.3 Results

Table 40 below provides results for the short-term dependencies of oil prices and the Tadawul index and its economic sectors. With respect to the existing literature, the findings on the TASI over the period 2007 to 2017 support the results of (Mensi, 2019; Alqattan & Alhayky, 2016; Samontaray, Nugali, & Sasidhar, 2014; Almohaimeed & Harrathi, 2013; Jouini, 2013) but contradict the findings of (Rahman, 2020; Akoum, Graham, Kivihaho, Nikkinen, & Omran, 2012; Fouquau, 2009). However, comparison is possible only to a limited extent, as these studies cover only a portion of the data and some use deviating short-term test methodologies and data frequencies.

Correlation with WTI*	Daily dataset	1st segment segment	2nd segment	3rd segment	4th segment	5th segment
TASI	0.1586	0.1569	0.1584	0.0911	0.1046	0.2310
Subindex 1	0.1321	0.1343	0.0983	0.1128	0.0839	0.2005
Subindex 2	0.1804	0.1418	0.1840	0.1156	0.1627	0.2858
Subindex 3	0.1302	0.1789	0.0759	0.0652	0.0350	0.1766
Subindex 4	0.1306	0.1595	0.1426	0.0223	0.0422	0.1824
Subindex 5	0.0963	0.1221	0.1015	-0.0228	0.0664	0.1503
Subindex 6	0.1125	0.1126	0.1552	0.0000	0.1038	0.1573
Subindex 7	0.1193	0.1556	0.1392	0.0592	0.0176	0.1491
Subindex 8	0.1489	0.1608	0.1305	0.0542	0.1203	0.2218
Subindex 9	0.1276	0.1628	0.1131	0.0427	0.0728	0.1793
Subindex 10	0.1395	0.1399	0.1653	0.0300	0.1047	0.1877
Subindex 11	0.1130	0.1447	0.0756	0.0056	0.0588	0.1739
Subindex 12	0.0844	0.1403	0.0666	0.0089	0.0690	0.0656
Subindex 13	0.0741	0.1268	0.1343	-0.0005	-0.0121	0.0599
Subindex 14	0.1362	0.1752	0.1550	0.0424	0.0263	0.1803
Subindex 15	0.0984	0.0999	0.0888	0.0146	0.1120	0.1484

* All estimates are statistically significant at the 1% level.

Table 40: Correlation results

Over the study period, the petro index returns show the highest correlation coefficient with crude oil returns. The aggregated index ranked second, which shows the strong influence of the petro sector on the stock index of Saudi Arabia. At ranks two and three, building and construction as well as industrial investment show high correlation with oil prices. In contrast, the lowest correlation is with media and publishing industries, followed by insurance and energy and utilities industries. These results are consistent with Mensi (2019). Although the rankings change the results of the first and second segments, they are comparable with the complete dataset, where individual rankings can be recognized in the selected economic sectors and overlapping timeframes of Jouini (2013) as well as Almohaimeed and Harrathi (2013). After the financial crisis, we find a significant decline in the short-term relation between crude oil prices and the TASI as well as with the respective economic sectors. For the economic sectors of insurance in the third segment and media and publishing in the third and fourth segments, the correlation coefficient is slightly negative. Although petro is still the most highly correlated economic sector, the relation with oil prices declines in the third segment but recovers in the fourth segment. The strongest correlation of WTI with the Tadawul is in the fifth segment. With minor exceptions, this is also true for the majority of economic sectors, where the known ranking order is evident.

Table 41 below shows the results for the long-term relation of oil prices with the Tadawul index and its economic sectors. In comparison with the literature, the findings on the TASI over the entire period 2007 to 2017 support the results of (Mensi, 2019; Alqattan & Alhayky, 2016; Jouini, 2013; Arouri, Jouini, Le, & Nguyen, 2012) but contradict the findings of (Rahman, 2020; Akoum, Graham, Kivihaho, Nikkinen, & Omran, 2012; Arouri & Rault, 2012; Arouri & Fouquau, 2011). As mentioned above, the comparison has only limited explanatory power, as this study utilizes the greatest possible time period of the Tadawul with 15 subindices, from 2007 to 2017, whereas previous research covers only segments of this timeframe.

Cointegration with WTI*	Daily dataset	1st segment	2nd segment	3rd segment	4th segment	5th segment
TASI	0.8848	0.1110	0.0010**	0.0281**	0.0029**	0.0225**
Subindex 1	0.5110	0.4381	0.0916	0.0082**	0.0034**	0.0603
Subindex 2	0.6240	0.0306**	0.0010**	0.0010**	0.0038**	0.0823
Subindex 3	0.9810	0.1310	0.0065**	0.1125	0.0030**	0.4017
Subindex 4	0.8572	0.0773	0.0209**	0.1497	0.0043**	0.0221**
Subindex 5	0.4014	0.0011**	0.1581	0.5902	0.0044**	0.0099**
Subindex 6	0.4412	0.1376	0.0068**	0.1002	0.0056**	0.3253
Subindex 7	0.9766	0.0728	0.7300	0.0868	0.0076**	0.3237
Subindex 8	0.1386	0.0582	0.1917	0.0010**	0.0010**	0.0372**
Subindex 9	0.8916	0.0736	0.3369	0.3896	0.0052**	0.0253**
Subindex 10	0.7879	0.3044	0.0025**	0.0692	0.0089**	0.0116**
Subindex 11	0.9035	0.0634	0.0081**	0.2876	0.0117**	0.0288**
Subindex 12	0.6249	0.1260	0.6394	0.0203**	0.0111**	0.8434
Subindex 13	0.5047	0.1475	0.7718	0.5097	0.0292**	0.7891
Subindex 14	0.9410	0.1453	0.0951	0.5721	0.0149**	0.0343**
Subindex 15	0.8064	0.1963	0.3651	0.5009	0.0029**	0.0047**

* P-value at r=0; ** Rejection at 5% level of significance.

Table 41: Cointegration results

Considering the complete timeframe, neither the TASI nor any economic sector is found to be cointegrated with crude oil. The results of the segmented datasets reveal a more heterogeneous pattern. In the first segment, which includes the period of the financial crisis, neither the TASI nor 13 out of the 15 economic sectors show significant co-movement in their returns. In the second and third segments, the TASI and six respectively four subindices show a long-term relation with oil prices, which is largely not consistent with the results of Jouini (2013). During the fourth segment, the TASI as well as all economic sectors exhibit long-range oil price dependency. This development decreases in the fifth segment, where the TASI, together with eight subindices, is cointegrated, which is, nevertheless, the second-most crude oil-dependent time period. Aggregating the five segmented periods, the TASI and the petro index in four out of five periods are cointegrated with crude oil prices, showing most significantly the long-term dependency of the Tadawul on WTI. In three out of five periods, retail as well as agricultural and food industries, together with the building and construction, industrial investment, and insurance sectors are long-term associated with oil prices. The least cointegrated and, therefore, most long-term oil-independent economic sectors are media and publishing as well as real estate development. Apart from the petro sector, these results deviate from Mensi (2019).

What both short- and long-term perspectives share is the increasing relation between oil prices and the Tadawul. Although the outcome is not consistent as in the case of correlation, the fifth segment shows the highest relation, and in the case of cointegration, the fourth segment is fully cointegrated while the fifth segment ranks second in terms of high oil price dependency, and the trend is significant. Further, the TASI and the economic sectors are, in their relative characteristics of oil price interaction, comparable in their short- and long-term behavior.

4.4 Conclusion

This paper analyzes the short- and long-term relation of crude oil prices with the Tadawul, with a distinct focus on economic sectors covering the longest possible time period of the Tadawul with 15 subindices, from 2007 to 2017, and providing insight on possible temporal development. We find significant long- and short-term relations between crude oil prices and the TASI as well as the petro sector, showing the high dependency of Saudi Arabia's economy on oil. Further, we generate empirical evidence from economic sectors such as media and publishing that are largely independent from oil price developments. Contrary to expectations, we find that, over time, the relation of the Tadawul to crude oil intensifies in both the short- and long-term. For investors, our results are of great importance, as global crude oil price fluctuations play a critical role in the world economy and especially in emerging and frontier markets (Mensi, 2019; Arouri & Rault, 2012).

The significant relation between oil prices and the Tadawul implies some degree of predictability (Arouri & Fouquau, 2011). In particular, portfolio diversification, asset allocation, arbitrage, and hedging strategies should be constructed differently when investors expect increasing or decreasing oil prices (Zhu, Li, & Li, 2014). Understanding the interdependencies between sectoral markets and oil prices allows investors to enhance diversification, risk hedging, and to seek investment opportunities differentiated according to the specific properties of each economic sector. In addition, the increasing relation between the Tadawul and crude oil prices suggests that the expected advantages of diversification from holding oil and stock sectors in Saudi Arabia are decreasing (Jouini, 2013). For policy makers, these results should enhance efforts toward diversifying the Saudi economy away from oil, reducing the reliance of the country on a single commodity. The importance of this undertaking is reflected by the ambitious National Transformation Program 2020 initiated by the Government of Saudi Arabia (Rahman, 2020).

This paper is not without limitations. Its academic validity could be enhanced by adding additional research methodologies, such as wavelet analysis or VEC models.

5. Concluding remarks

Collectively, these papers analyze the Tadawul from different perspectives, providing a thorough overview of the Saudi Stock Market. The key findings are as follows.

The quality of the financial market as measured by informational efficiency leaves possibilities for improvement. However, this provides opportunities for investors to outperform the market using active investment strategies. Further, the Tadawul is characterized by a high and increasing dependency on oil prices; this requires greater attention.

The first paper of the cumulative dissertation contributes to the inconclusive evidence collected on the weak-form market efficiency of the TASI, and especially of its subindices. In general, the efficient market hypothesis is a core proposition in the theory of finance with strong supporting empirical evidence (Risso, 2008); however, it has at the same time, always been a highly controversial topic (Sensoy, 2013). Stock market efficiency matters to academics in understanding the working mechanism and efficiency characteristics of equity markets, to investors in identifying and understanding investment opportunities, and to policy makers in developing the stock markets of emerging countries (Jamaani & Roca, 2015; Abdmoulah, 2010). Applying 12 parametric and nonparametric test methods, we show that the TASI and all its 15 subindices are not weak-form market efficient, but do not exhibit long-range dependency. Further, enhanced efficiency could not be documented in the time period 2007 to 2017, during which efficiency improves from the time of the financial crisis and declines during the period of recovery from the crisis. Theory and current literature provide a multiplicity of possible reasons for the absence of weak-form market efficiency in the Tadawul; these interact and to a great extent interrelate, for example, the presence of excessive stock market volatility and information asymmetry and the weak degree of foreign participation and high concentration in particular subindices, such as banking and petro (Jamaani & Roca, 2015). Further, the mean-reverting tendency of daily stock market returns and the herding behavior of the high proportion of domestic institutional investors (Bley, 2011), as well as the ineffectiveness and implementation difficulties of past reforms (Abdmoulah, 2010), play a significant role in the explanatory implications of the results.

The second paper connects two core topics of academic financial research: the weak-form market efficiency hypothesis and portfolio optimization (Maillard, Roncalli, & Teiletche, 2010; Lo, 2004). This is carried out via analysis of the feasibility of transforming the evident weak-form market inefficiency discovered in the Tadawul into risk-adjusted excess returns via application of quantitative techniques of portfolio optimization. This is implemented with the aim of empirically demonstrating the logical implication that inefficient markets are characterized by the ability of active investment strategies to outperform the market as a whole and to verify a direct link between the transformation magnitude and relative time and data frequency-dependent efficiency changes (Malkiel, 2003). These results matter to academics in understanding the interface between market efficiency and investment approaches in equity markets, to investors in identifying and understanding investment opportunities, and to policy makers (Jamaani & Roca, 2015). Applying a selection of quantitative asset allocation strategies to the 15 subindices of the TASI from 2007 to 2017 and benchmarking these results according to the selected set of measurement techniques against the index, this study shows that inefficiencies materialize as abnormal risk-adjusted returns that occur on a systemic and continuous basis. However, alignment of the ability to predict future prices from past price changes with a graduating degree of market efficiency is only partially traceable.

The third paper complements analysis of the Tadawul by investigating the relation between oil prices and the Tadawul in the time period 2007 to 2017. The test results from this paper are important to academics, investors, and policy makers in understanding the critical role of crude oil prices in the economy of Saudi Arabia, with a focus on individual economic sectors and possible temporal development. Applying Pearson's linear correlation coefficient to short-term co-movement and the Johansen cointegration test to long-term co-movement uncovers significant and strong relations between crude oil prices and the TASI, as well as the petro sector. Additionally, we generate empirical evidence from economic sectors that are to a great extent independent from oil price developments. Over time, the relation of the Tadawul and crude oil prices intensifies in the short- and long-term.

References

Abdmoulah, W. (2010). Testing the evolving efficiency of Arab stock markets. International Review of Financial Analysis, 19(1), 25–34.

Abraham, A., Seyyed, F. J., & Alsakran, S. A. (2002). Testing the random walk behavior and efficiency of the Gulf stock markets. Financial Review, 37(3), 469–480.

Ahlgren, P., Jarneving, B., & Rousseau, R. (2003). Requirements for a cocitation similarity measure, with special reference to Pearson's correlation coefficient. Journal of the American Society for Information Science and Technology, 54(6), 550–560.

Akoum, I., Graham, M., Kivihaho, J., Nikkinen, J., & Omran, M. (2012). Co-movement of oil and stock prices in the GCC region: A wavelet analysis. The Quarterly Review of Economics and Finance, 52(4), 385–394.

Al Abdulhadi, D., Shetty, S., & Alshamali, M. (2015). Stock market behavior: A fractal analysis of Saudi stock exchange. International Journal of Business, 20(1), 64–78.

Al-Abdulqader, K., Hannah, G., & Power, D. (2007). A test of the weak–form of the efficient markets hypothesis for the Saudi stock market. Journal of Emerging Market Finance, 6(2), 167–190.

Al-Ajmi, J., & Kim, J. (2012). Are Gulf stock markets efficient? Evidence from new multiple variance ratio tests. Applied Economics, 44(14), 1737–1747.

Al Ashikh, A. I. (2012). Testing the weak-form of efficient market hypothesis and the day-of-the-week effect in Saudi stock ex-

change: Linear approach. International Review of Business research papers, 8(6), 27–54.
Al Janabi, M. A., Hatemi-J, A., & Irandoust, M. (2010). An empirical investigation of the informational efficiency of the GCC equity markets: Evidence from bootstrap simulation. International Review of Financial Analysis, 19(1), 47–54.
Al-Khazali, O. M., Ding, D. K., & Pyun, C. S. (2007). A new variance ratio test of random walk in emerging markets: A revisit. Financial Review, 42(2), 303–317.
Alkholifey, A. A. (2001). The Saudi Arabian stock market: Efficient market hypothesis and investors' behavior. (Unpublished doctoral dissertation). PhD thesis, Colorado State University.
Almohaimeed, A., & Harrathi, N. (2013). Volatility transmission and conditional correlation between oil prices, stock market and sector indexes: Empirics for saudi stock market. Journal of Applied Finance and Banking, 3(4), 125–141.
Alqattan, A. A., & Alhayky, A. (2016). Impact of oil prices on stock markets: Evidence from gulf cooperation council (GCC) financial markets. Amity Journal of Finance, 1(1), 1–8.
Al-Razeen, A. M. (1997). The weak-form efficiency of the Saudi stock market (Unpublished doctoral dissertation). PhD thesis, University of Leicester.
Andrews, D. W. (1991). Heteroskedasticity and autocorrelation consistent covariance matrix estimation. Econometrica, 59(3), 817–858.
Anscombe, F. J. (1973). Graphs in statistical analysis. The American Statistician, 27(1), 17–21.
Arouri, M. E. H., & Fouquau, J. (2011). How do oil prices affect stock returns in GCC markets? An asymmetric cointegration approach. Bankers Markets & Investors: An Academic & Professional Review, 111, 5–16.
Arouri, M. E. H., Jouini, J., & Nguyen, D. K. (2012). On the relationship between world oil prices and GCC stock markets. Journal of

Quantitative Economics, 10, 98–120.

Arouri, M. E. H., & Rault, C. (2012). Oil prices and stock markets in GCC countries: Empirical evidence from panel analysis. International Journal of Finance & Economics, 17, 242–253.

Arshad, S., Rizvi, S. A. R., Ghani, G. M., & Duasa, J. (2016). Investigating stock market efficiency: A look at OIC member countries. Research in International Business and Finance, 36, 402–413.

Asiri, B., & Alzeera, H. (2013). Is the Saudi stock market efficient? A case of weak-form efficiency. Research Journal of Finance and Accounting, 4(6), 35–48.

Bachelier, L. (1900). Théorie de la spéculation. In Annales scientifiques de l'école normale supérieure (Vol. 17, pp. 21–86).

Ball, R., & Kothari, S. (1989). Nonstationary expected returns: Implications for tests of market efficiency and serial correlation in returns. Journal of Financial Economics, 25(1), 51–74.

Benjelloun, H., & Squalli, J. (2008). Do general indexes mask sectoral efficiencies? A multiple variance ratio assessment of Middle Eastern equity markets. International Journal of Managerial Finance, 4(2), 136–151.

Bera, A. K., & Park, S. Y. (2008). Optimal portfolio diversification using the maximum entropy principle. Econometric Reviews, 27(4-6), 484–512.

Bernardi, S., Leippold, M., & Lohre, H. (2018). Maximum diversification strategies along commodity risk factors. European Financial Management, 24(1), 53–78.

Bley, J. (2011). Are GCC stock markets predictable? Emerging Markets Review, 12(3), 217–237.

Box, G. E., Jenkins, G. M., Reinsel, G. C., & Ljung, G. M. (2015). Time series analysis: Forecasting and control. John Wiley & Sons.

Box, G. E., & Pierce, D. A. (1970). Distribution of residual autocorrelations in autoregressive-integrated moving average time series models. Journal of the American Statistical Association, 65(332), 1509–1526.

Bradley, J. V. (1968). Distribution-free statistical tests. Prentice-Hall.

Brown, R. M. (1988). A comparison of market efficiency among stock exchanges. Journal of Business Finance & Accounting, 15(3), 373–384.

Budd, B. Q. (2012). A "Random-walk" through the Saudi Arabian financial market: Is the Tadawul efficient? Journal of Finance and Accountancy, 10, 1–13.

Butler, K. C., & Malaikah, S. J. (1992). Efficiency and inefficiency in thinly traded stock markets: Kuwait and Saudi Arabia. Journal of Banking & Finance, 16(1), 197–210.

Campbell, J., Lo, A., & MacKinlay, A. (1997). The Econometrics of Financial Markets. Princeton University Press.

Cecchetti, S. G., & Lam, P.-S. (1994). Variance-ratio tests: Small-sample properties with an application to international output data. Journal of Business & Economic Statistics, 12(2), 177–186.

Charfeddine, L., & Khediri, K. B. (2016). Time varying market efficiency of the GCC stock markets. Physica A: Statistical Mechanics and its Applications, 444, 487–504.

Chaudhuri, K., & Wu, Y. (2004). Mean reversion in stock prices: Evidence from emerging markets. Managerial Finance, 29, 22–37.

Chaves, D., Hsu, J., Li, F., & Shakernia, O. (2011). Risk parity portfolio vs. other asset allocation heuristic portfolios. The Journal of Investing, 20(1), 108–118.

Chaves, D., Hsu, J., Li, F., & Shakernia, O. (2012). Efficient Algorithms for Computing Risk Parity Portfolio Weights. The Journal of Investing, 21(3), 150–163.

Choueifaty, Y., & Coignard, Y. (2008). Toward maximum diversification. The Journal of Portfolio Management, 35(1), 40–51.

Choueifaty, Y., Froidure, T., & Reynier, J. (2013). Properties of the most diversified portfolio. Journal of Investment Strategies, 2(2), 49–70.

Clarke, R., De Silva, H., & Thorley, S. (2013). Risk parity, maximum diversification, and minimum variance: An analytic perspective. The Journal of Portfolio Management, 39(3), 39–53.

Clausius, R. (1857). Ueber die Art der Bewegung, welche wir Wärme nennen. Annalen der Physik, 176(3), 353–380.

Cochrane, J. H. (1988). How big is the random walk in GNP? Journal of Political Economy, 96(5), 893–920.

Cohen, J. (1988). Statistical power analysis for the behavioral sciences. Erbaum Press, Hillsdale, NJ, USA.

Cont, R., Moussa, A., & Santos, E. (2013). Network structure and systemic risk in banking systems. Cambridge University Press.

Cootner, P. H. (1962). Stock prices: Ramdom vs. systematic changes. Industrial Management Review, 3(2), 24–45.

Couillard, M., & Davison, M. (2005). A comment on measuring the Hurst exponent of financial time series. Physica A: Statistical Mechanics and its Applications, 348, 404–418.

Croux, C., & Dehon, C. (2010). Influence functions of the Spearman and Kendall correlation measures. Statistical Methods & Applications, 19(4), 497–515.

Dahel, R., Laabas, B., et al. (1999). The behaviour of stock prices in the GCC markets. Economic Research Forum for the Arab Countries, Iran & Turkey.

DeFusco, R. A., McLeavey, D. W., Pinto, J. E., & Runkle, D. E. (2007). Quantitative investment analysis workbook. John Wiley & Sons.

DeMiguel, V., Garlappi, L., & Uppal, R. (2009). Optimal versus naive diversification: How inefficient is the 1/N portfolio strategy? The Review of Financial Studies, 22(5), 1915–1953.

DeMiguel, V., Martin-Utrera, A., & Nogales, F. J. (2013). Size matters: Optimal calibration of shrinkage estimators for portfolio selection. Journal of Banking & Finance, 37(8), 3018–3034.

Dent, W. T., & Cassing, S. (1978). On Durbin's and Sims' residuals in autocorrelation tests. Econometrica, 46(6), 1489–1492.

Dickey, D. A., & Fuller, W. A. (1979). Distribution of the estimators for autoregressive time series with a unit root. Journal of the American Statistical Association, 74(366a), 427–431.

Duchin, R., & Levy, H. (2009). Markowitz versus the Talmudic portfolio diversification strategies. The Journal of Portfolio Management, 35(2), 71–73.

Dufour, J.-M., & Dagenais, M. G. (1985). Durbin-Watson tests for serial correlation in regressions with missing observations. Journal of Econometrics, 27(3), 371–381.

Durbin, J., & Watson, G. (1950). Testing for serial correlation in least squares regression. Biometrika, 28, 409–428.

Engle, R. F., & Granger, C. W. (1987). Co-integration and error correction: Representation, estimation, and testing. Econometrica, 55, 251–276.

Engle, R. F., Granger, C. W., & Hallman, J. J. (1989). Merging short-and long-run forecasts: An application of seasonal cointegration to monthly electricity sales forecasting. Journal of Econometrics, 40(1), 45–62.

Engle, R. F., & Russell, J. R. (1998). Autoregressive conditional duration: A new model for irregularly spaced transaction data. Econometrica, 66, 1127–1162.

Evensky, H., & Evensky, H. R. (1997). Wealth Management: The Financial Advisor's Guide to Investing and Managing Client's Assets. New York: McGraw Hill.

Fabozzi, F. J., Focardi, S. M., & Kolm, P. N. (2006). Financial modeling of the equity market: From CAPM to cointegration (Vol. 146). John Wiley & Sons.

Fama, E. F. (1965). The behavior of stock-market prices. The Journal of Business, 38(1), 34–105.

Fama, E. F. (1970). Efficient capital markets: A review of theory and empirical work. The Journal of Finance, 25(2), 383–417.

Fama, E. F. (1998). Market efficiency, long-term returns, and behavioral finance. Journal of Financial Economics, 49(3), 283–306.

Fama, E. F., & French, K. R. (1988). Permanent and temporary components of stock prices. Journal of Political Economy, 96(2), 246–273.

Fernholz, R., Garvy, R., & Hannon, J. (1998). Diversity-weighted indexing. Journal of Portfolio Management, 24(2), 74–82.

Fieller, E. C., Hartley, H. O., & Pearson, E. S. (1957). Tests for rank correlation coefficients. I. Biometrika, 44(3/4), 470–481.

Fouquau, J. (2009). On the short-term influence of oil price changes on stock markets in GCC countries: Linear and nonlinear analyses. Economics Bulletin, 29, 795–804.

Fox, K. J. (1997). White noise and other experiments on augmented Dickey-Fuller tests. Applied Economics Letters, 4(11), 689–694.

Fugazza, C., Guidolin, M., & Nicodano, G. (2010). 1/N and long run optimal portfolios: Results for mixed asset menus. Federal Reserve Bank of St, Louis.

Fuller, W. A. (1976). Introduction to Statistical Time Series. New York: John Wiley.

Garlappi, L., Uppal, R., & Wang, T. (2007). Portfolio selection with parameter and model uncertainty: A multi-prior approach. The Review of Financial Studies, 20(1), 41–81.

Gosset, W. (1908). The probable error of a mean. Biometrika, 6, 1–25.

Granger, C. W. (1969). Investigating causal relations by econometric models and cross-spectral methods. Econometrica, 37, 424–438.

Griveau-Billion, T., Richard, J.-C., & Roncalli, T. (2013). A fast algorithm for computing high-dimensional risk parity portfolios. Available at SSRN 2325255, 1–9.

Guidi, F., & Gupta, R. (2013). Market efficiency in the ASEAN region: Evidence from multivariate and cointegration tests. Applied Financial Economics, 23(4), 265–274.

Habibagahi, H., & Pratschke, J. L. (1972). A comparison of the power of the von Neumann ratio, Durbin-Watson and Geary tests. The Review of Economics and Statistics, 54(2), 179–185.

Hallerbach, W. G. (1999). Decomposing portfolio value-at-risk: A general analysis. Journal of Risk, 5, 1–18.

Harris, R. I. (1992). Testing for unit roots using the augmented Dickey-Fuller test: Some issues relating to the size, power and the lag structure of the test. Economics Letters, 38(4), 381–386.

Hauke, J., & Kossowski, T. (2011). Comparison of values of Pearson's and Spearman's correlation coefficients on the same sets of data. Quaestiones Geographicae, 30(2), 87–93.

Hjalmarsson, E., & Österholm, P. (2010). Testing for cointegration using the Johansen methodology when variables are near-integrated: Size distortions and partial remedies. Empirical Economics, 39(1), 51–76.

Hokroh, M. (2013). An Application of the Weak Form of the Efficiency Hypothesis on the Saudi Arabia Stock Market after Tadawul. Asian Journal of Finance & Accounting, 5(1), 386.

Hurst, H. E. (1951). Long-term storage capacity of reservoirs. Trans. Amer. Soc. Civil Eng., 116, 770–808.

Jamaani, F., & Roca, E. (2015). Are the regional Gulf stock markets weak-form efficient as single stock markets and as a regional stock market? Research in International Business and Finance, 33, 221–246.

Jarque, C. M., & Bera, A. K. (1987). A test for normality of observations and regression residuals. International Statistical Review, 55, 163–172.

Jarrow, R. A., & Larsson, M. (2012). The meaning of market efficiency. Mathematical Finance: An International Journal of Mathematics, Statistics and Financial Economics, 22(1), 1–30.

Jensen, M. C. (1978). Some anomalous evidence regarding market efficiency. Journal of Financial Economics, 6(2/3), 95–101.

Jensen, M. C., & Benington, G. A. (1970). Random walks and technical theories: Some additional evidence. The Journal of Finance, 25(2), 469–482.

Jerome, M., & Well, A. (2003). Research design and statistical analysis.

Lawrence Erlbaum.
Jin, X. (2016). The impact of 2008 financial crisis on the efficiency and contagion of Asian stock markets: A Hurst exponent approach. Finance Research Letters, 17, 167–175.
Jobson, J. D., & Korkie, R. M. (1981). Putting Markowitz theory to work. The Journal of Portfolio Management, 7(4), 70–74.
Johansen, S. (1988). Statistical analysis of cointegration vectors. Journal of Economic Dynamics and Control, 12(2-3), 231–255.
Johansen, S. (1995). Identifying restrictions of linear equations with applications to simultaneous equations and cointegration. Journal of Econometrics, 69(1), 111–132.
Johansen, S. (2005). Interpretation of cointegrating coefficients in the cointegrated vector autoregressive model. Oxford Bulletin of Economics and Statistics, 67(1), 93–104.
Johansen, S., & Juselius, K. (1990). Maximum likelihood estimation and inference on cointegration—with appucations to the demand for money. Oxford Bulletin of Economics and Statistics, 52(2), 169–210.
Johansen, S., & Juselius, K. (2008). Allowing the data to speak freely: The macroeconometrics of the cointegrated vector autoregression. American Economic Review, 98(2), 251–55.
Jorion, P. (1986). Bayes-Stein estimation for portfolio analysis. Journal of Financial and Quantitative Analysis, 21, 279–292.
Jouini, J. (2013). Return and volatility interaction between oil prices and stock markets in Saudi Arabia. Journal of Policy Modeling, 35(6), 1124–1144.
J.P. Morgan. (1994). Riskmetrics technical document. New York.
Kan, R., & Zhou, G. (2006). Optimal estimation for economic gains: Portfolio choice with parameter uncertainty. Journal of Financial and Quantitative Analysis, 42, 621–656.
Kendall, M., & Stuart, A. (1973). The Advanced Theory of Statistics, Volume 2, Inference and Relationship. Griffin.
Kendall, M. G., & Hill, A. B. (1953). The analysis of economic time-

series-part I: Prices. Journal of the Royal Statistical Society. Series A (General), 116(1), 11–34.

Khababa, N. (1998). Behavior of stock prices in the saudi arabian financial market: Empirical reserach findings. Journal of Financial Management & Analysis, 11(1), 48–55.

Kolm, P. N., Tütüncü, R., & Fabozzi, F. J. (2014). 60 Years of portfolio optimization: Practical challenges and current trends. European Journal of Operational Research, 234(2), 356–371.

Kolusheva, D. (2008). Out-of-sample performance of asset allocation strategies. Available at SSRN 1802491, 1–31.

Kopman, L., & Liu, S. (2009). Maximizing the Sharpe Ratio and Information Ratio in the Barra Optimizer. MSCI Barra Research, 1–14.

Kremer, P. J., Talmaciu, A., & Paterlini, S. (2018). Risk minimization in multi-factor portfolios: What is the best strategy? Annals of Operations Research, 266(1-2), 255–291.

Kritzman, M., Page, S., & Turkington, D. (2010). In defense of optimization: The fallacy of 1/N. Financial Analysts Journal, 66(2), 31–39.

Ledoit, O., & Wolf, M. (2003). Improved estimation of the covariance matrix of stock returns with an application to portfolio selection. Journal of Empirical Finance, 10(5), 603–621.

Ledoit, O., & Wolf, M. (2004a). Honey, I shrunk the sample covariance matrix. The Journal of Portfolio Management, 30(4), 110–119.

Ledoit, O., & Wolf, M. (2004b). A well-conditioned estimator for large-dimensional covariance matrices. Journal of Multivariate Analysis, 88(2), 365–411.

Leote de Carvalho, R., Lu, X., & Moulin, P. (2012). Demystifying equity risk–based strategies: A simple alpha plus beta description. The Journal of Portfolio Management, 38(3), 56–70.

Lintner, J. (1965). Security prices, risk, and maximal gains from diversification. The Journal of Finance, 20(4), 587–615.

Liu, X. (2014). Portfolio Selection via Shrinkage by Cross Validation. Journal of Finance and Accounting, 2(4), 74–81.

Ljung, G. M., & Box, G. E. (1978). On a measure of lack of fit in time series models. Biometrika, 65(2), 297–303.

Lo, A. W. (1991). Long-term memory in stock market prices. Econometrica, 59, 1279–1313.

Lo, A. W. (2004). The adaptive markets hypothesis. The Journal of Portfolio Management, 30(5), 15–29.

Lo, A. W., & MacKinlay, A. C. (1988). Stock market prices do not follow random walks: Evidence from a simple specification test. The Review of Financial Studies, 1(1), 41–66.

Lo, A. W., & MacKinlay, A. C. (1999). A non-random walk down Wall Street. Princeton University Press.

Lohre, H., Opfer, H., & Orszag, G. (2014). Diversifying risk parity. Journal of Risk, 16(5), 53–79.

Maillard, S., Roncalli, T., & Teïletche, J. (2010). The properties of equally weighted risk contribution portfolios. The Journal of Portfolio Management, 36(4), 60–70.

Malhotra, N., Tandon, K., & Tandon, D. (2015). Testing the Empirics of Weak Form of Efficient Market Hypothesis: Evidence from Asia-Pacific Markets. IUP Journal of Applied Finance, 21(4), 18–37.

Malkiel, B. G. (2003a). The efficient market hypothesis and its critics. Journal of Economic Perspectives, 17(1), 59–82.

Malkiel, B. G. (2003b). Passive investment strategies and efficient markets. European Financial Management, 9(1), 1–10.

Mandelbrot, B. (1966). Forecasts of future prices, unbiased markets, and martingale models. The Journal of Business, 39(1), 242–255.

Mandelbrot, B. (1972). Statistical methodology for nonperiodic cycles: from the covariance to R/S analysis. In Annals of Economic and Social Measurement, Volume 1, Number 3 (pp. 259–290). NBER.

Mandelbrot, B. B., & Taqqu, M. S. (1979). Robust R/S analysis of long run serial correlation. IBM Thomas J. Watson Research Division.

Marashdeh, H. (2017). Oil price shocks and stock market returns in the three largest oil-producing countries. International Journal of Energy Economics and Policy, 7(5), 312-322.

Markowitz, H. (1952). Portfolio Selection. The Journal of Finance, 7(1), 77–91.

Markowitz, H. (1991). Portfolio Selection: Efficient diversification of investments. Malden: Blackwell-Publishers.

Mensi, W. (2019). Global financial crisis and co-movements between oil prices and sector stock markets in Saudi Arabia: A VaR based wavelet. Borsa Istanbul Review, 19(1), 24–38.

Mensi, W., Tiwari, A. K., & Yoon, S.-M. (2017). Global financial crisis and weak-form efficiency of Islamic sectoral stock markets: An MF-DFA analysis. Physica A: Statistical Mechanics and its Applications, 471, 135–146.

Meucci, A. (2009). Managing diversification. Risk, 22, 74–79.

Meucci, A., Santangelo, A., & Deguest, R. (2015). Risk budgeting and diversification based on optimized uncorrelated factors. Risk, 11, 70–75.

Michaud, R. O. (1989). The Markowitz optimization enigma: Is 'optimized' optimal? Financial Analysts Journal, 45(1), 31–42.

Molgedey, L., & Ebeling, W. (2000). Local order, entropy and predictability of financial time series. The European Physical Journal B-Condensed Matter and Complex Systems, 15(4), 733–737.

Morey, M., & Vinod, H. (2001). A Double Sharpe Ratio. In C. Lee (ed.). Advances in Investment Analysis and Portfolio Management, 8, 57–66.

Moskowitz, T. (2000). Discussion. The Journal of Finance, 55, 1695–1703.

Murphy, J. J. (1999). Technical analysis of the financial markets:

A comprehensive guide to trading methods and applications. Penguin.

Newey, W., & West, K. (1987). A simple, positive semi-definite, heteroskedasticity and autocorrelation consistent covariance matrix. Econometrica, 55(3), 703–708.

Onour, I. A. (2004). Testing weak-form efficiency of Saudi stock exchange market. Ministry of Economy and Planning, Riyadh: Saudi Arabia, 1–14.

Onour, I. A. (2009). Testing efficiency performance of Saudi stock market. Journal of King Abdulaziz University: Economics and Administration, 23(2), 15–27.

Osborne, M. F. (1962). Periodic structure in the Brownian motion of stock prices. Operations Research, 10(3), 345–379.

Pearson, K. (1920). Notes on the history of correlation. Biometrika, 13(1), 25–45.

Phillips, P. C. (1987). Time series regression with a unit root. Econometrica, 55, 277–301.

Phillips, P. C., & Perron, P. (1988). Testing for a unit root in time series regression. Biometrika, 75(2), 335–346.

Poddig, T., Brinkmann, U., & Seiler, K. (2005). Portfoliomanagement: Konzepte und Strategien. Bad Soden: Uhlenbruch.

Poddig, T., Dichtl, H., & Petersmeier, K. (2008). Statistik, Ökonometrie, Optimierung: Methoden und ihre praktischen Anwendungen in Finanzanalyse und Portfoliomanagement. Bad Soden: Uhlenbruch.

Radcliffe, R. C. (1987). Investment: Concepts, analysis, strategy. London: Scott, Foresman and Company.

Rahman, A., et al. (2020). Long run Association of Stock Prices and Crude Oil Prices: Evidence from Saudi Arabia. International Journal of Energy Economics and Policy, 10(2), 124–131.

Regnault, J. (1863). Calcul des chances et philosophie de la bourse. Paris: Mallet-Bachelier and Castel.

Risso, W. A. (2007). A randomness test for financial time series. Revista de Economía, 14(1), 155–176.

Risso, W. A. (2008). The informational efficiency and the financial crashes. Research in International Business and Finance, 22(3), 396–408.

Risso, W. A. (2009a). The informational efficiency: The emerging markets versus the developed markets. Applied Economics Letters, 16(5), 485–487.

Risso, W. A. (2009b). Measuring the informational efficiency in the Stock Market. Retrieved from http://homepage.sns.it/marmi/lezioni/talk_risso.pdf.

Rodgers, J., & Nicewander, W. A. (1988). Thirteen ways to look at the correlation coefficient. The American Statistician, 42(1), 59–66.

Roncalli, T., & Weisang, G. (2016). Risk parity portfolios with risk factors. Quantitative Finance, 16(3), 377–388.

Said, S. E., & Dickey, D. A. (1984). Testing for unit roots in autoregressive-moving average models of unknown order. Biometrika, 71(3), 599–607.

Samontaray, D. P., Nugali, S., Sasidhar, B., et al. (2014). A study of the effect of macroeconomic variables on stock market: Saudi Perspective. International Journal of Financial Research, 5(4), 120–127.

Samuelson, P. (1965). Proof that properly discounted present values of assets vibrate randomly. Industrial Management Review, 6(2), 41–49.

Saudi, S., Exchange. (2016). Home. Retrieved from https://www.tadawul.com.sa/wps/portal/tadawul/home.

Saudi, S., Exchange. (2017). New Industry Classification. Retrieved from https://www.tadawul.com.sa/wps/portal/tadawul/knowledge-center/about/new-industry-classification.

Savin, N. E., & White, K. J. (1977). The Durbin-Watson test for serial correlation with extreme sample sizes or many regressors. Econometrica: Journal of the Econometric Society, 45(8), 1989–1996.

Sensoy, A. (2013). Generalized Hurst exponent approach to efficiency in MENA markets. Physica A: Statistical Mechanics and its Applications, 392(20), 5019–5026.

Shalan, S. A. B., & Ykhlef, M. (2015). Solving multi-objective portfolio optimization problem for Saudi Arabia stock market using hybrid clonal selection and particle swarm optimization. Arabian Journal for Science and Engineering, 40(8), 2407–2421.

Shannon, C. E. (1948). A mathematical theory of communication. The Bell System Technical Journal, 27(3), 379–423.

Shapiro, M. D., Blanchard, O. J., & Lovell, M. C. (1986). Investment, output, and the cost of capital. Brookings Papers on Economic Activity, 1986(1), 111–164.

Sharpe, W. F. (1966). Mutual fund performance. The Journal of Business, 39(1), 119–138.

Sharpe, W. F. (1994). The sharpe ratio. Journal of Portfolio Management, 21(1), 49–58.

Spearman, C. (1904). The proof and measurement of association between two things. The American Journal of Psychology, 15(1), 72–101.

Stoyanov, S. V., Rachev, S. T., & Fabozzi, F. J. (2007). Optimal financial portfolios. Applied Mathematical Finance, 14(5), 401–436.

Taylor, B. (2006). MathWorks News & Notes - October 2006 - Developing Portfolio Optimization Models. Retrieved from The MathWorks: `www.mathworks.com/mason/tag/proxy.html?dataid=8272`.

Tsay, R. S. (2005). Analysis of financial time series (Vol. 543). John Wiley & Sons.

Tu, J., & Zhou, G. (2011). Markowitz meets Talmud: A combination of sophisticated and naive diversification strategies. Journal of Financial Economics, 99(1), 204–215.

Wald, A., & Wolfowitz, J. (1940). On a test whether two samples are from the same population. The Annals of Mathematical Statistics, 11(2), 147–162.

Weber, C. E. (2001). F-tests for lag length selection in augmented Dickey–Fuller regressions: Some Monte Carlo evidence. Applied Economics Letters, 8(7), 455–458.

Wolf, M. (2004). Resampling vs. shrinkage for benchmarked managers. Institute for Empirical Research in Economics-University of Zurich, 1–15.

Yu, J.-R., Lee, W.-Y., & Chiou, W.-J. P. (2014). Diversified portfolios with different entropy measures. Applied Mathematics and Computation, 241, 47–63.

Zakaria, N., & Hashim, F. (2017). Emerging Markets: Evaluating Graham's Stock Selection Criteria on Portfolio Return in Saudi Arabia Stock Market. International Journal of Economics and Financial Issues, 7(2), 453–459.

Zhu, H.-M., Li, R., & Li, S. (2014). Modelling dynamic dependence between crude oil prices and Asia-Pacific stock market returns. International Review of Economics & Finance, 29(C), 208–223.

FSC
www.fsc.org
MIX
Papier | Fördert gute Waldnutzung
FSC® C083411

Kolibri 360 GmbH
Ferdinand-Jühlke-Straße 7
99095 Erfurt, Deutschland
produktsicherheit@kolibri360.de